Dedicated to Heather Sinard, who came to us as a nanny, but ended up a dear friend and sister in the Gospel. I never could have written this without you.

A letter to leaders:

Thank you for your willingness to lead this study. Leading a Bible study can be intimidating. If you are like me, the unknowns are the most frightening. I never know what kind of questions will be asked. Someone might dominate the group. Conflicts could arise. I do not know how well the group members will connect with the material, with each other or with me. I do not like feeling out of control.

But there is good news for fearful leaders. Jesus does not want us to try to impress him with our courage or competence. Instead, he invites us to humbly admit our need for his wisdom and presence. As leaders, we ought to be the first to come to Jesus and discover for ourselves that he is a gentle Savior. Then the heavy burden of needing to control the outcome of this study can be replaced with the assurance that he is working out his purposes in the lives of all those in the group, including the leader. (Matthew 11:28-30)

It is so easy to dilute the Gospel. Our desire to earn God's favor through our own merit is insatiable. In order to keep the truth of the Gospel in focus, I have included a separate page of objectives and theological concepts for each chapter.

Before you begin, please be sure that you have recruited at least one prayer partner for yourself. Keep in close contact, praying as specifically as you can. Jesus longs to gather each of us under his wing. His heart for sinners encourages us to pray boldly. God bless you as you lead your group!

Under His Smile,

Sue Cortese

Certain sins are easy to recognize. Others can be overlooked or even considered virtuous. For example, the desire to become an independent, competent Christian is a dangerous sin. But it is often encouraged by volumes of books offering formulas for personal success. This is deadly. Jesus promises to meet us in our neediness, but we would rather have no needs. We prefer earning heaven's applause to needing a Savior. The Apostle Paul showed how this desire works against the Gospel.

What then shall we say that Abraham, our forefather, discovered in this matter? If, in fact, Abraham was justified by works, he had something to boast about—but not before God. What does the Scripture say? "Abraham believed God, and it was credited to him as righteousness."

Now when a man works, his wages are not credited to him as a gift, but as an obligation. However, to the man who does not work but trusts God who justifies the wicked, his faith is credited as righteousness (Romans 4:1-5).

These verses were written to Christians. They are in the present tense. Every day we need to believe in the God who justifies wicked people like us. Then, like Abraham, we can be continually amazed at the gift of God's unmerited favor.

Modern Christian teaching often denies the depth of sin that still resides in our hearts. Yet, any honest look within will reveal a shocking degree of self-centeredness. When we are exposed we try to cleanse our conscience by resolving to change. But these verses tell us that we must refuse to work for our righteousness. We must not try to cover our shame with our performance.

The goal of UNDER HIS SMILE is to reveal the beauty of the Gospel, where wicked people are given the free gift of Christ's perfect record and are received by their heavenly Father with a warm embrace. The answer to our deep insecurity is not self improvement. Christian growth is not measured by our increasing ability to handle life's problems with competence and power. Instead it is measured by our increasing realization of our need for Jesus. God resists the proud performer, but gives grace to the humble.

This is such a foreign concept to most Christians that it will have to be discussed many times. That is what this study attempts to do: repeat the Gospel to Christians until we begin to grasp the good news.

MEDITATION QUESTIONS:

The meditation exercises are central to the course. Dr. Timothy Keller explains that we will remain merely insightful about our sin until we learn how to meditate on Scripture. We sin because we naturally trust our own ideas about how life works more than we trust God. Unless we pay careful attention to what God has said we will not abandon our natural coping strategies. Therefore, encourage your group to spend time daily on the meditation verses.

In the leader's guide I have given my personal answers for the first set of meditation questions. Feel free to make copies and give them to the members of your group. Encourage everyone to begin as early in the week as possible. It does not matter whether they answer one question per day or whether the entire exercise is done in one sitting. The value is found in taking time to ponder what God has said, letting his truth transform our hearts.

Some of the meditation questions may be new for your group. They are designed to expose unbelief and its destructive consequences. Then they point to Jesus. Jesus was a perfect example of obedience that comes from faith. The truth of any verse is seen in his life. But it is Jesus' death that saves us. The following is a key meditation question and may need to be explained to your group.

How is Jesus' death on the cross the ultimate payment for this sin or need of mine?

It is critical to know that Jesus has made full payment for all our sin by his death on the cross. Our natural instinct is to promise God and ourselves that we will do better, rather than to remember the body and blood of Jesus. He told us to remember. Most people need help understanding what Jesus did for us on the cross. The Leader's guide notes for chapter nine discuss the cross in more detail and may help you explain its centrality.

Expect God to work through the meditation questions. This is what he has promised:

*Now to him who is able to do
immeasurably more than all we ask or imagine,
according to his power that is at work within us,
to him be glory in the church and in Christ Jesus
 throughout all generations, for ever and ever! Amen.*
Ephesians 3:20, 21

A friend of mine is a psychologist. One of her first clients was a twelve-year-old girl diagnosed with schizophrenia.

"Before we begin," the girl said, "I have something for you."

She reached into her bag and pulled out a magic wand she had made. "Here. Now you can fix me!"

My friend has kept that wand. It reminds her of the deep longing so many of us have. We want a magical "cure" that will fix us.

Why do we feel the need to be better people than we are? Perhaps you can think of several ways that you need to change, and change quickly! Maybe you think you are failing the people who need you the most. You might feel like you are your own worst enemy, ruining your life on a daily basis. It can seem like a better "you" is the ticket to your own happiness and the happiness of those you love. It can also seem like the ticket to a better relationship with God.

Consider the following two questions:

→ How satisfied are you with your current level of spiritual maturity?

→ In light of that, how does God feel about you right now?

A MATTER OF APPROVAL

What would it be like to know that we already have the approval of the only One whose opinion matters? What if we knew that this One, who created the universe, is actively involved in carrying out his plan for our lives and that his plan is good, to bless us and not to harm us? What if we grasped that his will toward us is kind, and that every moment we are under his smile?

There is so much we need to know about God. What is he like? Can we trust him? How can we know for sure? Unfortunately, it often feels too risky to let go of our commitment to our own plans and strategies in order to learn about God. Our need to perform feels more urgent than our need to know and trust God. So we work to improve, to impress and to succeed. But we are never as good as we pretend to be. We never will be in this life. There is no magic wand, no self-help program, and no training regimen that can bring us the cure that we long for. Instead, the way to genuine transformation begins by asking God to free us from the need to perform. We must put the magic wand back in the bag, and ask God to open our eyes so we can see the One who earned for us the permanent smile of his Father.

Our problem is that we crave approval. Letting go of the need to become admirable and praise-worthy is easier said than done. Imagine going a whole day without contemplating the impression you are making on others. Try to go a week without making a single excuse or boast. Then attempt to live a few waking hours without comparing yourself to others, or mentally excusing your faults or failures. We cannot do it. We have become addicted to performance and appearance as the way of obtaining what we think we need in life. It will take more than inspiring words to liberate us. We need a rescue from above. Rose Marie Miller compares our helpless condition to that of a caterpillar in a ring of fire.

> *Here then is my theme: the only hope of liberation for a helpless, resisting caterpillar in a ring of fire is deliverance from above. Someone must reach down into the ring and take us out… this is not supporting grace, but transforming grace.*

Thanks be to God, we have a Rescuer! His Name is Jesus. We cannot change ourselves, but he can change us from the inside out. In this course, we go back to Eden to see where our drive to perform began, and to learn why it is so powerful. Then we study God's rescue and the freedom that Jesus won for us. Finally, we consider what a life free of performance and pretense looks like, and how we can begin to live this way.

Meditation

You are likely to cover familiar ground as you work through this study. The purpose of the course is to move the truth from your head to your heart. While we need to understand the Bible and reason out what it teaches, we cannot stop there. If it is going to change our desires and the object of our trust, the truth must reach our heart. This can happen when we spend time with a verse, pondering it prayerfully and considering its impact on our lives.

Dr. Timothy Keller, the pastor of Redeemer Presbyterian Church in New York City, researched how Christians from the past meditated upon the Bible. Men such as Martin Luther and John Wesley would contemplate a passage verse-by-verse, sometimes even word-by-word. Dr. Keller compiled a list of questions from their writings that are helpful for us today. Meditation is not a process that takes hours or that seeks to drill a truth into our lives through mindless repetition. Instead it is a simple process of learning to ask key questions that engage our core beliefs and ambitions. At the end of each chapter there is a meditation section using Dr. Keller's questions. Real change and freedom are offered to us in the Gospel. We can expect God to transform us as we meditate on his Word!

Prayer

Do you know someone who would be willing to pray for you as you work through this course? Ask this friend to be your prayer partner for the next twelve weeks. What we need the most is the ability to hear God. Jesus repeatedly cried out, "He who has ears to hear, let him hear." Very few heard him. Why? What they already "knew" kept them from hearing what Jesus had to say. We are prone to the same deafness. Ask your prayer partner to pray that the Holy Spirit would give you "ears to hear" what God is telling you in his Word. Try to talk regularly so you both can see how God is listening and answering.

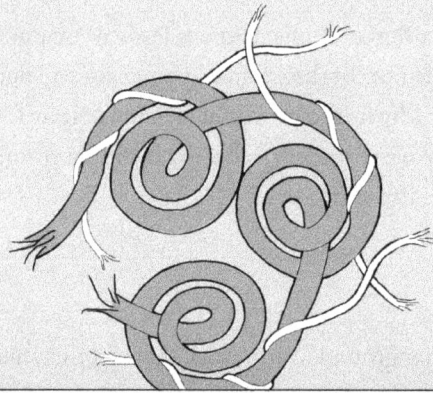

PART ONE ❖ THE PROBLEM

OBJECTIVES:

1. *To realize the need to look beneath behavior.*

Jesus chided the Pharisees for reducing obedience to a list of behaviors (Luke 11:39, Matthew 15: 7-20). Everything we do and say comes from our heart. When we sin, the problem is not our behavior. We need to uncover the beliefs and longings that lead us to do what we do. Adam and Eve did not have a problem with fruit grabbing. They ate the forbidden fruit because they began to believe something new about God and themselves. Their belief led to new longings for things that were outside God's will.

Unless we understand the dynamic behind our sinful behavior, we will never truly change.

Every sin comes from believing something that is not true.

Before we can grasp the true nature of sin, we have to understand the truth about God, ourselves and the world in which we live. Therefore, several chapters in this study are devoted to learning about God, Adam and Eve, Paradise, and the Serpent who deceived them. In every chapter, we will be seeking to understand the heart and motives of everyone involved.

2. *To grasp the centrality of trusting God's heart.*

God knows that we will never obey him if we do not love him. His first and greatest commandment is that we love him with all our heart, soul, strength and mind (Matthew 22:37). If he simply wanted to control our behavior, God would never have demanded that our whole being be fully engaged in loving him. We cannot perform that kind of love. We cannot be coerced into it. We must be won.

How can the God of the Bible win our hearts? Too often he is viewed as the analyzer of our behavior, but not the lover of our soul. Such a god could never capture our affection. If we do not believe that God's love for us is sincere and passionate, we cannot trust him. But, when we realize that his heart is filled with the kind of love that we have longed for, we will begin to freely give him our hearts. The first chapter is dedicated to revealing the beauty of God's love.

THEOLOGICAL CONCEPTS

1. *The Trinity.*

No other religion has a triune god. Apart from Christianity, monotheistic religions worship a one-person god. If god existed as one person only, he would have lived alone until he began to create. God would not have loved until he had someone to love. Even then, all of his relationships would be condescending, limited to inferior beings, like the love a man feels for his dog. This kind of deity may be viewed as generous and kind, but not as a god of love.

In polytheism, where many individual gods are worshipped, genuine love does not exist. Usually, the gods are characterized by the worst sins of humanity. They can be bribed and manipulated. They deceive and seek revenge. Polytheistic deities are not gods of love.

In Christianity alone, love is central to God's nature. The Bible reveals that "God IS love." (1 John 4:7,8). He is the "Father of compassion and the God of all comfort" (2 Corinthians 1:3). Love comes before creation. From all eternity, the Father, the Son and the Holy Spirit loved each other with passion and sincerity (John 17:24-26). The triune God was never lonely or deficient in any way. Creation is the result of the overflow of God's love, not the need for love. Joy, not emptiness, led the Father, the Son and the Holy Spirit to create us.

Jesus came to bring us back into the circle of the perfect love of God (John 15:9). Because God is a Trinity, we can receive from the Father, the Son and the Holy Spirit, the incredible love that has always flowed between them. In our age of cynicism, we can rest in the certainty of love, which has existed from all eternity. Love is the greatest of all virtues. It will endure forever and never fail (1 Corinthians 13:8, 13).

2. *God's glory.*

God's glory is his "weight" or his worthiness. Sometimes God's glory is described as the bright cloud of his presence (Exodus 24:16, 17). Moses asked God to show him his glory. But God told him that he could not see his face and live (Exodus 33:20). When Jesus was transfigured on the mountain, his glory was revealed. "His clothes became as bright as a flash of lightning" (Luke 9: 29). Then a cloud descended and the disciples fell on their faces in fear.

From these accounts we learn that God exists in the unbearable brightness of glory. We often act as if God has little "weight" or glory. We diminish his awesome worth and prefer to think of him as a friend or kind hearted old man. Yet if God were to reveal his glory to us we would perish. Even Jesus, after his ascension, was terrifying when he appeared to his beloved disciple, John. John described his experience: "His face was like the sun shining in all its brilliance. When I saw him, I fell at his feet as though dead" (Revelation 1:16, 17).

God does not terrorize us out of a desire to humiliate or shame us. Instead, he wants us to know him as he is. He is worthy of worship and holy fear. We need to know his glory so that we do not glorify lesser things.

God's glory is also revealed in his creation (Psalm 19:1-4; Romans 1:18-21). It can be life changing to take time pondering the truth that God created all that exists simply through his spoken command.

There is another way that God's glory is revealed. God loves sinners, outcasts and rebels.

Though he is holy, just and powerful, he is full of mercy and compassion for those who bring him nothing but their need. Isaiah captures the glory of God's greatness and his condescension.

This is what God the LORD says:
he who created the heavens and stretched them out,
who spread out the earth and all that comes out of it,
who gives breath to its people,
and life to those who walk on it:
"I, the LORD, have called you in righteousness;
I will take hold of your hand.
I will keep you and will make you
to be a covenant for the people
and a light for the Gentiles,
to open eyes that are blind,
to free captives from prison
and to release from the dungeon those who sit in darkness.
"I am the LORD; that is my name!
I will not give my glory to another
or my praise to idols.
Isaiah 42:5-8

The one "called in righteousness" is Jesus, God in the flesh, who gave his life to bring us back to his Father. God wants us to know that he loves sinners. He wants to open our blind eyes, set us free from our prisons, and take us from darkness into light. He really does love us!

When we lose sight of the glory of God we look for glory in empty places. We die of thirst. But when we comprehend the glory of the real God, we find ourselves full of living water. His glory alone can fill our thirsty souls.

"Has a nation ever changed its gods?
(Yet they are not gods at all.)
But my people have exchanged their Glory
for worthless idols.
Be appalled at this, O heavens,
and shudder with great horror,"
declares the LORD.
"My people have committed two sins:
They have forsaken me,
the spring of living water,
and have dug their own cisterns,
broken cisterns that cannot hold water."
Jeremiah 2:11-13

Perfectionism is a cancer that permeates our modern culture. A twelve-year-old girl described it well: "It used to be that all you needed to be was pretty. Now you have to be pretty, smart and athletic!" You do not have to be young to feel overwhelmed by impossibly high standards. All of us feel pressure to be better than we are, and to live better than we do. Unfortunately, the modern Christian message has not lightened our burden or brought us rest. Instead it has raised the bar. It is not enough to be competent. We need to be like Jesus!

But perfectionism is not from God. It has another source. Strangely enough, this ambition was first embraced by a woman who had no reason to seek self-improvement. The God who created her saw that she was "very good." Her husband loved her as she was, and she loved him. She lived in an unspoiled Paradise and felt no shame. Her name was Eve. She had it all, and it was not enough.

During the next few weeks we will look carefully at Paradise and the fall of Adam and Eve. Hopefully, you will gain new insights into what went wrong. First, we need to do some background work on the characters involved and the world in which they lived. Let's begin with God.

God is the Creator of the heavens and the earth.

> **GENESIS 1:10**   God called the dry ground "land," and the gathered waters he called "seas." And God saw that it was good.
> **GENESIS 1:12**   The land produced vegetation: plants bearing seed according to their kinds and trees bearing fruit with seed in it according to their kinds. And God saw that it was good.
> **GENESIS 1:18**   ...to govern the day and the night, and to separate light from darkness. And God saw that it was good.
> **GENESIS 1:21**   So God created the great creatures of the sea and every living and moving thing with which the water teems, according to their kinds, and every winged bird according to its kind. And God saw that it was good.
> **GENESIS 1:25**   God made the wild animals according to their kinds, the livestock according to their kinds, and all the creatures that move along the ground according to their kinds. And God saw that it was good.
> **GENESIS 1:31**   God saw all that he had made, and it was very good. And there was evening, and there was morning — the sixth day.

Each day of Creation concludes with: "And God saw that it was _____*good*_____."

After the sixth day of creation God added a word to his verdict: "God saw all that he had made, and it was _____*very good*_____."

In Genesis, God uses the brief, precise language that scientists love. As his newly created world burst with life and beauty, and as the sky shimmered with billions of stars, God simply said, "Good."

But this is not the only account of creation.

> *I was appointed from eternity, from the beginning, before the world began.*
> *I was there when he set the heavens in place,*
> *when he marked out the horizon on the face of the deep,*
> *when he established the clouds above*
> *and fixed securely the fountains of the deep,*
> *when he gave the sea its boundary*
> *so the waters would not overstep his command,*
> *and when he marked out the foundations of the earth.*
> *Then I was the craftsman at his side.*
> *I was filled with delight day after day,*
> *(or And I was daily his delight,)*
> *rejoicing always in his presence, rejoicing in his whole world*
> *and delighting in mankind.*
> PROVERBS 8:23, 27-31

Commentators explain that Jesus is the one speaking. These verses paint a picture of a father and son working side by side as master craftsmen.

→ What did the Father feel toward his Son?
Delight

→ How did the Son feel about working with his Father?
He was rejoicing always in his Father's presence.

→ How did the Son feel about what they had made?
He rejoiced in his whole world.

→ What filled the Son's heart as he looked at mankind?
Delight

Our joy is made complete when we share it with someone we love. The Father's joy was full because his Son was at his side. The Son's delight in mankind was magnified by his Father's presence. There was another Person present at creation.

GENESIS 1:2   Now the earth was formless and empty, darkness was over the surface of the deep, and the Spirit of God was hovering over the waters.

The Holy Spirit shared in the joy of Creation.

Comprehending the Trinity — one God, three persons — is beyond our ability. However, the Trinity reveals that relationship is central to God's identity. Before anything was created, God is love (1 John 4:8). God created because he loved. And love was poured into everything that the Father, the Son and the Holy Spirit made.

Do you know God as He really is?
   · the Father, the Son and the Holy Spirit
   · rejoicing in each other's presence,
   · filled with delight in each other
   · and in all that each one does,
   · delighting in the man and the woman, created in their image.

➜ What difference would it make if you knew God in this way?
   (*Our view of God is the most important thing about us. As you lead this discussion you may want to ask your group how they tend to picture God. Follow with an analogy of a child with a parent. If the parent is quick tempered or uninvolved, how would the child relate to him or her? What difference would it make if the parent is genuinely happy and filled with love for the child? Apply this to the way we would approach God if we believed that he is full of joy and takes great delight in us.*)

Adam and Eve surely knew God's joy and pleasure. Imagine seeing God's eyes filled with pure delight as he looks at you! This is what Adam and Eve experienced. Not only did they know his love, but they also knew his glory.

> *This is what God the LORD says —*
> *he who created the heavens and stretched them out,*
> *who spread out the earth and all that comes out of it,*
> *who gives breath to its people,*
> *and life to those who walk on it:*
> *"I am the LORD; that is my name!*
> *I will not give my glory to another*
> *or my praise to idols."*
> ISAIAH 42:5, 8

➜ What has God alone done?

   He alone created the heavens and spread out the earth. He alone gives us breath and life.

➜ Whose glory does God refuse to give to another? *His own glory.*

God alone is God. He will not be anything less to us than God. His love for Adam and Eve was all the more beautiful because it came from a holy, powerful, and all wise God. How do you view God? Do you know his delight, his glory? Read each question below and mark the response that matches your perceptions of God. Try to avoid giving the "right" answers.

	Not at all	A little	Completely
How powerful is God?			
How crucial is God to every relationship you have and every situation you face?			
How beautiful is God?			
How joyful is the Trinity?			
How deeply does God care about you?			
How involved is God in your struggles?			
How tangible is God, how much difference does his presence make?			
How willing is God to help you?			
How helpful is God's help?			
How good are God's ideas concerning what is best for you and those you love?			
How well does God know you?			
How much does your life matter to God?			

Read each question again and this time answer with the word "completely."
This is the truth about God!

➔ How would your life be different if you knew God well enough to answer "completely" for every question?
Answers will vary.

God loves being God. He loves being your God. No one loves you like your Creator! No one has the glory of your Creator!

MEDITATION

God often seems far away and unconcerned about our problems. We tend to think that we are pursuing him and he is not responding. The verses below reveal just the opposite. God is pursuing us and we are not listening. We would rather trust in our own efforts than in him. But when we resist God we miss out on what he alone can give us.

> *This is what the Sovereign LORD, the Holy One of Israel, says: "In repentance and rest is your salvation, in quietness and trust is your strength, but you would have none of it."*
> ISAIAH 30:15

> *Yet the LORD longs to be gracious to you;*
> *he rises to show you compassion.*
> ISAIAH 30:18

Use the meditation questions that follow to contemplate Isaiah 30:18 during the week.

PRAYER

The written prayer is an aid to talking with your Father. Feel free to use it or to offer your own prayer instead.

Father,

The Bible reveals that you are filled with joy and delight. I don't often picture you that way when I pray. Usually I picture you far away and uninterested in my small life and its insignificant details. I find it hard to believe that you love me. But you say that you love me enough to pursue me. You want to give me grace and compassion.

I am not sure I even know how to respond to you. As I contemplate this verse, help me to understand and believe your words. I want to repent and rest. I want to receive your gifts.

In Jesus' name,
Amen.

Yet the LORD longs to be gracious to you;
he rises to show you compassion.

ISAIAH 30:18

REFLECT ON THE TEACHING

What is it saying? (Put this verse in your own words.)

The Lord wants me to know that He cares and is with me in my suffering. He yearns for me to know his favor, which he freely gives. When I am suffering he wants me to turn to him, instead of running to another source of comfort. He knows that he, alone, can give me what I need.

WORSHIP

What have I learned that I can praise God for?

God actually gets up to show us compassion. It is overwhelming to realize that the God who spoke the universe into being is a God who longs to show us his grace and compassion. This is a God I can be real with. I can come to him when I am at my worst. He wants me to come. He does not want to shame me or pay me back for all I've done to him. Instead, he is the father of the prodigal. He gets up and runs to me, reassuring me of his favor with a warm embrace and extravagant gifts.

REPENTANCE

How do I fail to realize this truth in my life?

Most of the time I think that God is irritable or impatient with me. I am afraid that he is as frustrated with me as I am with myself. If he were to rise, it would not be to show me compassion. Instead it would be to show me all my faults and to let me know how I need to improve.

What am I like when I forget this truth?

(What do I feel? How do I act? How do I treat God and others?)

When I forget, I feel condemned for my many failures and sins. I try to ward off accusation by working to measure up in some way. I try to bring God a better heart, more faith, or a better attitude. But I cannot keep it up. So I escape into a book, or a movie, or some form of mindless entertainment. When I forget, I treat God as if he were an abusive parent who demands what I will never be able to give. I put demands on my husband and children to come through for me so I can look good. I work to impress important people so that they can give me a favorable verdict. I do not love anyone and end up anxious, critical, driven and tired.

THANKFULNESS FOR A SAVIOR

How is Jesus the ultimate example of someone who lived out the truth of this verse?
Jesus never doubted his Father's grace and compassion. Therefore, Jesus was always full of grace. He loved his Father and was moved with compassion when he saw suffering of any kind. His compassion for sinners led him to die on a cross in our place. By his life and death, Jesus proved that this verse is true.

How is Jesus' death on the cross the ultimate payment for this sin or need of mine?
When Jesus hung on the cross he was wearing my willful unbelief. The One who treasured his Father's compassion was treated like one who despised it. Jesus received the rejection that I deserve and won for me the favor that he deserves. Because of the cross, I am received by my Father as if I had never resisted his grace or spurned his compassion.
The only answer for my sin is the cross where Jesus died in my place. God knows the pride and ingratitude behind my rejection of his grace and compassion. Yet he loves me so deeply that he did not spare his only Son.
I desperately need God's grace and compassion. The cross assures me that I have both.

ASPIRATION

How does this verse show me what I should be or do?
This verse shows me that I should receive the grace that God gives me so freely in Christ. I should trust his compassion which is vividly revealed at the cross. I should look long and hard at the cross and never forget the price God paid to show me favor. When life seems hard or unfair, I should let God into my suffering, and trust his heart. Since he is gracious and compassionate, I do not have to hide my real feelings or fears. I should talk to him about everything and trust him to love me well.

How would I be different if this truth were powerfully real to me? (Ask God for it!)
I would love my Father. I would listen when he tells me he loves me. I would look for his mercy every day. I would trust his heart, not my own. Therefore I would not strive to make my heart good enough for him, but would let his grace and compassion transform me. I would care more about my children knowing the grace of God, then learning how to act as if they did not need it. I would want others, even my enemies, to know the beauty of God's love for sinners. I would long for them to receive the grace and compassion I have received.

OBJECTIVES

1. *To consider the beauty of Adam and Eve's relationship with God.*

We live in an age where authority is suspect. History reveals how badly it has been abused. Those in power tend to take advantage of people under them, whether in the work place, the family, or in the larger arena of government. The abuse of power has led many to reject the authority of God. We want the power to decide who God is and what he wants from us. But deep down, we know that God can't be forced into our mold.

Yet, we are afraid of God's authority. In order to get beyond our fear, we must look carefully at mankind's unspoiled relationship with God. In Genesis we see God exercising the kind of rule that we long for. He created an incredible world and handed it over to Adam and Eve to rule. He did not micromanage or oppress them. Instead he gave them his blessing. He seemed to take great pleasure in watching them exercise the authority he gave them. God loved Adam and Eve. Under his rule they were elevated, blessed and free to take real dominion over a perfect world. God's authority is exercised in love.

2. *To show the greatness of Adam and Eve before they sinned.*

We are not biological accidents in an empty universe. We have a Creator who made us in his image. Adam and Eve were brilliant, fearless and loving. The glory of our original creation ought to inspire us. But there is another reason to grasp the greatness of the sinless man and woman.

Adam and Eve are often viewed as innocent victims of the Serpent. We resist believing that they willingly and knowingly turned away from God for a bite of forbidden fruit. A bumper sticker expresses our natural inclination: "Eve was framed!" We tend to equate sinlessness with naivety. Since Adam and Eve had no experience with evil, we might think that they were incapable of dealing with temptation.

But, Adam and Eve were not less mature than we are. Sin inhibits our intelligence and keeps us from reaching our potential. Adam and Eve were stunning in their sinlessness. They may not have comprehended evil, but they were wise enough to know that the Serpent was slandering God's character. Listening to the Serpent was all the more tragic because they knew God's love so intimately.

We have to be careful about our natural desire to be victims rather than sinners. A recent conversation illustrates this tendency:

"You know," a woman told me, "Eve was like a toddler. She couldn't have known what she was doing when she ate the fruit. It was not her fault."
"I have never known sin to make anyone a wiser, more mature person." I replied. "Eve must have been the most intelligent woman who has ever lived. She knew enough to know she was betraying God. It was her fault."
"Well, I'm not the sort of person who likes to criticize others" she said.

"You don't understand," I said. "I have to know that God loves guilty women, or else I will never know that he loves me."

The only reason we want to exonerate Eve, is that we want to exonerate ourselves. If Adam and Eve were too naïve to resist the Serpent, then it is God's fault that sin entered the world. This view appeals to our desire for innocence, but it does not address our deepest need. We are sinners. We long to be loved by someone who knows the worst about us yet still loves us. We do not have to blame God for our sinfulness. His love is designed for sinners. Jesus came for the people we really are, not the people we pretend to be. "For I have not come to call the righteous, but sinners" (Matthew 9:13).

It is hard to imagine what Adam and Eve were like. In their sinless perfection, how were they different from us? What was it like to see God in person and to live in Paradise?

Last week we looked at the love and joy of the Trinity spilling over into creation. In the first two chapters of Genesis we see how that delight expressed itself.

> GENESIS 1:26-31   Then God said, "Let us make man in our image, in our likeness, and let them rule over the fish of the sea and the birds of the air, over the livestock, over all the earth, and over all the creatures that move along the ground." So God created man in his own image, in the image of God he created him; male and female he created them. God blessed them and said to them, "Be fruitful and increase in number; fill the earth and subdue it. Rule over the fish of the sea and the birds of the air and over every living creature that moves on the ground." Then God said, "I give you every seed-bearing plant on the face of the whole earth and every tree that has fruit with seed in it. They will be yours for food. And to all the beasts of the earth and all the birds of the air and all the creatures that move on the ground — everything that has the breath of life in it — I give every green plant for food." And it was so. God saw all that he had made, and it was very good. And there was evening, and there was morning — the sixth day.

Only Adam and Eve were created in God's image.

➜ What do you think were their unique qualities, which set them apart from the animals?
Adam and Eve were able to think, to feel, to make choices, and to love in ways that reflected the nature of the God who created them.

➜ What did God give to Adam and Eve before he called them to rule over his newly created world?
God gave them his blessing.

➜ Why do you think God did that first?
Answers will vary. God did not only impart to Adam and Eve the ability to fulfill their high calling, but he also gave them his smile. Adam and Eve could move forward with confidence and joy.

➜ What did God give them to do?
Adam and Eve were to fill the earth and rule over everything God had made.

Adam and Eve were God's representatives, given the highest position in his newly created world.

➜ What did God relinquish in order to give Adam and Eve dominion?
God gave up his right to make all the decisions . He called Adam and Eve to take real dominion over the world he made. They had the freedom to make plans and carry them out.

Sometimes we picture Adam and Eve as toddlers in adult bodies. Everything was new for them and evil was unknown. Yet innocence does not imply inability or immaturity. Consider how capable Adam and Eve actually were.

> GENESIS 2:19-20   Now the LORD God had formed out of the ground all the beasts of the field and all the birds of the air. He brought them to the man to see what he would name them; and whatever the man called each living creature, that was its name. So the man gave names to all the livestock, the birds of the air and all the beasts of the field.

Think about the care that goes into the giving of a name. Expectant parents take months to find just the right name for their unborn child. Names have to "fit."

➜ Who alone has the right to name another?
The one who assumes the responsibility to care and provide for the other's needs

➜ Whom did God appoint to name the animals he had created?
Adam

➜ What does this tell us about Adam's calling and his ability to fulfill it?
In order to name all the animals, Adam would need to be able to identify their main characteristics. He also had to remember the names he had given! In addition, he had genuine authority over the animals and the responsibility of caring for them. He must have been incredibly intelligent, capable and wise.

➜ How did God help Adam with this task?
God brought the animals to Adam.

➜ How final was Adam's decision about each animal's name?
Whatever Adam called an animal, that became its name.

➜ What does this reveal about God's leadership style with Adam?
God let Adam make real choices and did not interfere. The wording seems to suggest that God enjoyed the process. He waited to see what name Adam would choose, like a proud parent watching his child display his talents.

Some of us are better at delegating important tasks than others. It is hard to give up control, especially if we care about the outcome. Notice how freely God gave Adam full control over his task. You sense that God is enjoying himself as he watches Adam come up with each new name. Just as the Son delighted in His Father's work, God now delights in Adam's work.

Let's look at Eve.

GENESIS 1:27   So God created man in his own image; in the image of God he created him; male and female he created them.

➜ Did Adam, by himself, reflect the image of God?
No. Adam and Eve, male and female, reflect the image of God.

GENESIS 2:18, 21-25   The LORD God said, "It is not good for the man to be alone. I will make a helper suitable for him." So the LORD God caused the man to fall into a deep sleep; and while he was sleeping, he took one of the man's ribs and closed up the place with flesh. Then the LORD God made a woman from the rib he had taken out of the man, and he brought her to the man. The man said, "This is now bone of my bones and flesh of my flesh; she shall be called 'woman,' for she was taken out of man." For this reason a man will leave his father and mother and be united to his wife, and they will become one flesh. The man and his wife were both naked, and they felt no shame.

➜ Who said that it was not good for Adam to live alone?
God said that it was not good.

➜ Whose idea was it to create woman?
It was God's idea.

➜ What kind of helper did God want Adam to have?
Someone who was "suitable" for him.

The word "suitable" literally means "corresponding." The term reflects both Eve's similarity to Adam, having also been made in the image of God, and her capability to make up for what he lacked. Adam would no longer be alone. Think about the characteristics Eve must have possessed in order to be a match for Adam.

➜ What does her suitability tell us about Eve?
Eve had to be an intelligent, capable woman or Adam would have remained lonely. She was similar to him, sharing God's image. Yet her femininity complemented his masculinity. She was similar, yet opposite.

➜ God presented Eve to Adam. What ceremony does this resemble?
God escorted Eve to meet Adam. This resembles marriage where the father of the bride escorts his daughter to her new husband.

➜ What does God intend for a man and a woman to become when they unite in marriage?
God intends for the two individuals to become "one flesh."

The Trinity is One God, but three persons. Now Adam and Eve are one flesh, but two persons.

➔ How does their union reveal the image of the God?
As each member of the Trinity delights in the other, so Adam and Eve delighted in each other. God exists in three persons, but the unity is so complete that God is One. Adam and Eve are two individuals who are so united as to become one flesh.

There is a single sentence that speaks volumes about the relationship that Adam and Eve enjoyed. Verse 25 tells us that they were "naked, and they felt no shame." Try to imagine a marriage with no shame and no shaming. Try to imagine a world without fear and shame.

➔ What does this reveal about Adam and Eve's love for each other?
Adam and Eve were totally at ease with each other. They trusted each other and were wholly trustworthy.

Ponder for a moment how wonderfully God made Adam and Eve. Were they simple and naïve? Think about each quality listed below. Were Adam and Eve inferior or superior to us?

- · Leadership ability.
- · Intelligence.
- · An intimate knowledge of those under their rule.
- · Genuine and healthy unity in marriage.
- · Enjoyment of each other's differences.
- · Ability to know and love each other without contempt.
- · Willingness to be known without spin or cover.
- · Ability to love and be loved.

Sin never brings growth, but immaturity. Sin never enlarges a soul, but always shrinks it. Adam and Eve were glorious in their sinlessness. They were intelligent, fearless, and loving. They received God's blessings freely and boldly tackled the high calling they were given. They were pleased with each other, having no shame or inclination to shame the other. Adam and Eve reflected the glory of their Creator, and his image was clearly revealed in all that they did.

MEDITATION

Although we are far from what Adam and Eve were, we still bear the image of our Creator. The One who made us has not forgotten us. We are on his mind! Take time to reflect on the Creator who made us in his image. We matter to him!

> *When I consider your heavens,*
> *the work of your fingers,*
> *the moon and the stars,*
> *which you have set in place,*
> *what is man that you are mindful of him,*
> *the son of man that you care for him?*
> PSALM 8:3, 4

PRAYER

Father,

When I look at Adam and Eve, I realize what you created us to be. I see brilliant minds, sinless love, and the freedom of being naked and unashamed. I see a marriage that reflected the joyful love of the Trinity -- both unity and diversity being celebrated. I see Adam and Eve assuming their roles as rulers and caretakers for the earth and all living things. The high position you assigned Adam and Eve reveals your gracious love for them and your confidence in their abilities. This is what you created men and women to be. Open my eyes to the greatness of being made in your image.

In Jesus' name,
Amen.

What is man that you are mindful of him,
the son of man that you care for him?
PSALM 8:4

REFLECT ON THE TEACHING

What is it saying? (Put this verse in your own words.)

WORSHIP

What have I learned that I can praise God for?

REPENTANCE

How do I fail to realize this truth in my life?

What am I like when I forget this truth?
(What do I feel? How do I act? How do I treat God and others?)

THANKFULNESS FOR A SAVIOR

How is Jesus the ultimate example of someone who lived out the truth of this verse?

How is Jesus' death on the cross the ultimate payment for this sin or need of mine?

ASPIRATION

How does this verse show me what I should be or do?

How would I be different if this truth were powerfully real to me? (Ask God for it!)

OBJECTIVES

1. *To know that God's work is beautiful.*

Our hearts naturally distrust God. We hang onto our plans, our loved ones, and our possessions because we are afraid of him. He seems to be the kind of ruler who sends people "gifts" like poverty, sickness or abandonment. We fear that his plan for us involves taking away more than giving.

But God can only give precious gifts of great value. He is the Author of genuine beauty and sincere love. Unfortunately, our appetites have become distorted so that we value short lived pleasures more than God's eternal gifts. The longer we live, the more we realize that the prizes we have coveted fall far short of bringing the fulfillment we expected. The beautiful home, the promotion, our achievements, the achievements of our children, none of these bring us the deep joy, peace and satisfaction we long for.

God always brings beauty into our lives. Paradise was beautiful. He does not prefer black and white to color, or monotony and ugliness to creativity and variety. Creation itself reveals the breathtaking beauty of God, from sunrises to rainbows, from snow capped mountains to fields of wild flowers. We can joyfully turn everything over to God and expect "beauty instead of ashes, the oil of gladness instead of mourning, and a garment of praise instead of despair" (Isaiah 61:3).

THEOLOGICAL CONCEPT

Work

God knows the blessing of work. We reflect his image when we use his creation creatively. From art to mathematics, from gardening to architecture, from seeking new knowledge to teaching what one has learned, we reveal the God who made us by using our gifts freely and joyfully. Each of us knows the pleasure of a job well done. It is the curse that makes work a burden, not work itself. When we can work at something we enjoy, in the company of people we love, we are truly happy.

Heaven is often depicted as a world of clouds where everyone is reclining and either eating grapes or strumming a harp. Many of us fear that we will be eternally bored. But our Creator knows what brings us deep satisfaction. We will not spend eternity on a cloud, but on a totally renewed earth (Isaiah 65:17, 66:22; 2 Peter 3:13; Revelation 21:1). We will be free from everything that makes our current work a burden. In a perfect world, we will joyfully serve the God who has won our hearts (Revelation 22:3).

We know that the Garden of Eden was beautiful.

➔ As you imagine Adam and Eve living there, what do you picture them doing?
Answers will vary.

➔ Where is God?
Answers will vary. God is often pictured as a ray of light descending from the sky.

Let's look at Paradise.

> GENESIS 2:4-16   This is the account of the heavens and the earth when they were created. When the LORD God made the earth and the heavens — and no shrub of the field had yet appeared on the earth and no plant of the field had yet sprung up, for the LORD God had not sent rain on the earth and there was no man to work the ground, but streams came up from the earth and watered the whole surface of the ground — the LORD God formed the man from the dust of the ground and breathed into his nostrils the breath of life, and the man became a living being. Now the LORD God had planted a garden in the east, in Eden; and there he put the man he had formed. And the LORD God made all kinds of trees grow out of the ground — trees that were pleasing to the eye and good for food. In the middle of the garden were the tree of life and the tree of the knowledge of good and evil. A river watering the garden flowed from Eden; from there it was separated into four headwaters. The name of the first is the Pishon; it winds through the entire land of Havilah, where there is gold. (The gold of that land is good; aromatic resin and onyx are also there.) The name of the second river is the Gihon; it winds through the entire land of Cush. The name of the third river is the Tigris; it runs along the east side of Asshur. And the fourth river is the Euphrates. The LORD God took the man and put him in the Garden of Eden to work it and take care of it. And the LORD God commanded the man, "You are free to eat from any tree in the garden..."

➔ How was the garden watered?
A river flowed through Eden watering the garden.

→ Describe the trees that God caused to grow.
There were all kinds of trees that were beautiful and good for food.

→ What could be found in Havilah?
Gold of high quality could be found, as well as aromatic resin and onyx.

→ What do these verses reveal about our Creator?
God is an accomplished artist, and everything he creates is beautiful, useful and good.

→ What was Adam supposed to do in the garden?
Adam was supposed to work the garden and take care of it.

→ Did you picture Adam and Eve working in Paradise? Why or why not?
Answers will vary.

We are made in God's image. Therefore we enjoy meaningful work. Yet, work on earth is saddled with pain. Imagine working in paradise without the "thorns" of pride, envy, greed, impatience, and fear. Imagine working under God's smile, free from accusation or contempt. Paradise was the place where God's image bearers were free to develop and use their gifts.

→ What kind of work do you love? What work gives you more energy than it takes away?
Answers will vary.

➜ Imagine doing that work in Paradise. What would you love to do in a perfect world?
  Answers will vary.

GENESIS 3:8   The LORD God... was walking in the garden in the cool of the day...

➜ What form was God taking when he visited Adam and Eve?
  He appears to be taking the form of a man.

Sometimes we visualize God's presence in Eden as a ray of light descending from the clouds. But Genesis reveals that God was walking to meet Adam and Eve.

➜ What is the difference between taking a walk with God in a garden, and hearing God's voice booming down from the sky?
  God's presence would not frighten Adam and Eve. Instead, intimacy and friendship is implied. (This verse refers to God's coming after the fall. Yet the wording seems to suggest that God had come to them in this way before.)

➜ What images does the phrase "cool of the day" bring to your mind?
  Answers will vary. At the very least is feels like something pleasant and comfortable.

Imagine God coming to meet with you in the coolness of the day in Paradise.

➜ If you were to take a walk with him, what might you want to talk about?
  Answers will vary.

We long for beauty. Not just in our world, but in our hearts. God is the author of beauty. We were created to live in a world pleasing to our eyes, in relationships that are pleasing to our souls, and with work that enables us to bring pleasure to others. We long for the beauty that Adam and Eve knew. We long for their freedom and joy. We do not know how long Adam and Eve enjoyed Paradise. They must have remembered it their whole lives.

MEDITATION

Although our world barely resembles Paradise, and we barely resemble Adam and Eve, God is still as beautiful as ever. He brings beauty into our fallen world and into our fallen hearts.

> *Praise the LORD, O my soul,*
> *and forget not all his benefits —*
> *who satisfies your desires with good things*
> *so that your youth is renewed like the eagle's.*
> PSALM 103:2, 5

PRAYER

Father,

The world you created was beautiful. If you had created monotony and boredom, Adam and Eve might have longed for something more. If you had been distant and uncaring, their fall might be easier to explain. But you are great enough to create wonder in our hearts, yet gentle enough to walk with us in a garden.

You alone can satisfy my desires with good things. Your beauty fills my soul when I seek you. Give me the grace to draw near to you and let you give me your best gifts!

In Jesus' name,
Amen.

Praise the LORD, O my soul,
and forget not all his benefits—
who satisfies your desires with good things
so that your youth is renewed like the eagle's.

PSALM 103:2, 5

REFLECT ON THE TEACHING

What is it saying? (Put this verse in your own words.)

WORSHIP

What have I learned that I can praise God for?

REPENTANCE

How do I fail to realize this truth in my life?

What am I like when I forget this truth?
(What do I feel? How do I act? How do I treat God and others?)

Thankfulness for a Savior

How is Jesus the ultimate example of someone who lived out the truth of this verse?

How is Jesus' death on the cross the ultimate payment for this sin or need of mine?

Aspiration

How does this verse show me what I should be or do?

How would I be different if this truth were powerfully real to me? (Ask God for it!)

OBJECTIVE

1. *To understand the subtlety of temptation.*

It is "tempting" to view Satan as an obvious menace whose main work is to posses human souls or entice them to commit immoral acts. But the devil's ordinary way of working is much more subtle. He is crafty and deceptive. He has the ability to appear kindhearted and thoughtful at the very time he is trying to pull us away from Christ and those we love.

We hear inner voices all the time. For example, after a conflict we tend to replay every word that was spoken in an attempt to figure out who was right and who was wrong. Sometimes a soothing voice is heard. It might come from our own mind, or from a well meaning friend. This voice assures us that we are not the problem. We are victims of God or others. We have been misunderstood! No one has loved us the way we deserve to be loved. We begin to believe lies about the conflict. The result is separation, bitterness and pain. This kindhearted voice ultimately comes from the enemy.

We are naturally self centered (James 1:13-15). Yet our tendency toward selfish ambition, envy, self pity and self righteousness is always eager to be encouraged by the subtle, lying Serpent (James 3:14-16). Because he is a liar and a murderer, Satan wants us to stay deceived, at war with others and cut off from the God who loves us.

Satan not only entices us to sin, he also harasses our conscience through accusation (Revelation 12:10). Our drive to perform is often an attempt to silence the condemnation we feel. The devil can even tempt us to renew our commitment to serve Christ. He lures us to try to cover our guilt through works instead of going to the cross.

This may be a new thought for many in your group. If we spend our lives working hard at being good enough for God, the end result will be self-deception and separation. We will never feel at peace with God this way. Either we will demand that God accept our works or we will become angry with him for making it so hard to please him. Others will feel our defensiveness and pride, and will want to remain at a distance. We have been utterly deceived by the devil at the very time we thought we were serving God.

Satan is very subtle and none of us realize how deceived we are. This is why meditation on Scripture is so vital to our spiritual well being. God always tells the truth. His goal for us is life and reconciliation. We can resist the devil when we are "firm in the faith" (1 Peter 5:9). When we allow God's promises to become more vivid than our fears, the devil ends up fleeing from us (James 4:7). When we know the truth, Satan's devices are easier to recognize (2 Corinthians 2:11).

THEOLOGICAL CONCEPTS

1. *Satan's origin and existence.*

Our culture is beginning to change its mind about evil and an ultimate evil being. We have witnessed too many inexplicable atrocities to reduce evil to psychological factors. The Bible teaches that there is an evil one who is the source of all oppression, injustice, deception and murder.

From the Bible we learn that the devil has existed since the beginning of time (1 John 3:8). We know that he is a created being, since God is the Creator of everything that exists. From Job 1: 6 we learn that Satan presented himself before God with the angels. Like all angels, he must answer God's questions and receive God's permission before he can do his work. The authority he exercises has been given to him (Luke 4:6). He is called the 'ruler of this world' (John 14:30) and the ruler of the kingdom of the air' (Ephesians 2:2). He is the prince of demons and has a kingdom with malicious servants who carry out his will (Matthew 12:24-28).

We may end up with more questions than answers as we read the biblical accounts of Satan. Why would God allow such an evil being to exist and do so much harm to those he loves? How did Satan become evil in the first place? Where did evil come from?

God does not answer all our questions. But we do know that the defeat of Satan cost the suffering and death of his only Son (1 John 3:8; Hebrews 2:14). God has not subjected us to anything that he was not willing to bear himself. The only reason Jesus endured such pain was to release us from the dominion of Satan and bring us home to live in his kingdom forever.

Satan is not all powerful or eternal. Through Jesus we have been set free from Satan's rule and from the eternal death that is awaiting the devil and all those who serve him.

2. *God's Sovereignty and Satan's activity.*

The Bible is clear that Satan has to ask God for permission to act (Job 1:12; 2:6). When we see evil up close we cannot imagine why God would allow it. The book of Job tackles this question head on. Job endured horrific suffering at the hands of Satan, but with permission from God. Perhaps the end of the book gives us insight. Satan's purpose in tormenting Job was to prove that he was unfaithful at heart. He was Job's accuser and wanted to see him curse God to his face.

God is not like Satan. His purposes are redemptive. His plan was to reveal his surpassing greatness to Job. After a season of terrible pain (physical, emotional, spiritual and relational) Job got his one desire. He took his complaint to God and heard his response. God did not give Job an explanation, but rather exposed him to a crash course on the difference between God and man. It could seem like an added assault to a man already crushed. But Job ended up healed and in awe of God. He condemned himself and worshipped God.

"I know that you can do all things;
no plan of yours can be thwarted.
You asked, 'Who is this that obscures my counsel without
knowledge?'
Surely I spoke of things I did not understand,
things too wonderful for me to know.
"You said, 'Listen now, and I will speak;
I will question you,
and you shall answer me.'
My ears had heard of you
but now my eyes have seen you.
Therefore I despise myself
and repent in dust and ashes."

Satan loves to work evil, yet his operations end up working for good in those who belong to God. As Joseph told his brothers, "You intended to harm me, but God intended it for good" (Genesis 50:20). In every case, Satan enjoys bringing evil. But God uses evil for good.

The ultimate example is the cross. As Jesus anticipated the suffering he was about to endure, he could say with confidence, "Now is the time for judgment on this world; now the prince of this world will be driven out. But I, when I am lifted up from the earth, will draw all men to myself" (John 12:31,32). Satan could not resist murdering the Son of God when he had the opportunity. Yet, even as he caused Judas to betray Jesus and stirred up the authorities against him, Satan was causing the destruction of his own kingdom. His act of ultimate evil ended up bringing about the reconciliation of sinners to God.

God freely gave Adam and Eve everything on the earth to enjoy, except for the fruit from one particular tree. God forbade them to eat from the tree of the knowledge of good and evil. Let's look at the verses that describe this command.

> GENESIS 2:15-17   The LORD God took the man and put him in the Garden of Eden to work it and take care of it. And the LORD God commanded the man, "You are free to eat from any tree in the garden; but you must not eat from the tree of the knowledge of good and evil, for when you eat of it you will surely die."

Consider all we have read from Genesis chapters one and two. Fifty-four verses are devoted to describing the beauty of creation, Adam and Eve, and God's relationship with them. The limitations that God placed upon them only take up two verses.

➔ What does this show us about the emphasis God placed on rules?
God placed more emphasis on blessing Adam and Eve than on giving them rules to obey.

➔ What did God say would happen to Adam and Eve if they ate from the forbidden tree?
They would surely die.

What kind of tree was the tree of the knowledge of good and evil? It sounds like something from a fairy tale. But the tree was real and so was its fruit. The Bible tells us a little about the tree.

> GENESIS 2:8, 9   Now the LORD God had planted a garden in the east, in Eden; and there he put the man he had formed. And the LORD God made all kinds of trees grow out of the ground — trees that were pleasing to the eye and good for food. In the middle of the garden were the tree of life and the tree of the knowledge of good and evil.

➔ What were all the trees like?
They were all beautiful and full of good fruit.

→ Where was the tree of the knowledge of good and evil?
It was in the center of the garden.

→ What tree was next to it?
The tree of life.

God did not give Adam and Eve the reason for his command, or explain why the punishment was so severe. In the next chapter we will see how the Serpent took advantage of God's silence and offered his own interpretations.

God is God. He does whatever he pleases. The good news is that what pleases him is always wise, loving and just. His ways are so unlike ours. Sometimes God can appear to be anything but wise and loving.

→ What might God want from us when we do not understand what he is doing?
God wants us to trust him, not his plan.

Keeping God's command did not require great skill or moral achievement on Adam and Eve's part. They were free to eat the fruit from all the trees in the garden. Every tree was as appealing to the eyes as the forbidden tree, and every fruit good for food. They could eat to their heart's content from every tree but one.

→ What would their obedience cost them?
It would not cost Adam and Eve anything to obey God. They had plenty to eat and to enjoy.

→ What would their obedience show to God?
They would be showing trust and loving submission to him as their Creator.

➜ If they broke this command, what would they be refusing to show God?
They would be refusing to show him love, submission and trust.

➜ What does this reveal about the purpose of the command?
The purpose of the command was to give Adam and Eve the opportunity to submit willingly to their Creator out of love and trust.

The Pharisees placed supreme value on moral achievement. They made all sorts of rules to measure their own obedience. But Jesus saw through them.

> MATTHEW 15:7, 8   You hypocrites! Isaiah was right when he prophesied about you: "These people honor me with their lips, but their hearts are far from me."

➜ What did the Pharisees pretend to do?
They pretended to honor God.

➜ Where were their hearts?
Their hearts were far from God.

We can perform without trust or submission. We can perform to hide our rebellion. God did not command Adam and Eve to perform; he gave a simple command.

Think about the nature of submission.

➜ What kind of person might you submit to willingly — even joyfully?
Someone who is wise, who loves me and is committed to what is best for me.

➜ What kind of relationship did God want with Adam and Eve?
God wanted a relationship based upon trust. He wanted Adam and Eve to believe that he loved them and was worthy of their trust and obedience.

Have you ever wondered why God did not warn Adam and Eve that Satan was in the Garden? Why did he allow them to face the Serpent on their own, with no warning? Good parents never leave their children alone in dangerous situations. But Adam and Eve were not children. They were intelligent adults. They knew God and understood his command.

➜ Why do you think God might have left Adam and Eve alone to encounter the Serpent?
God gave Adam and Eve the opportunity to choose the one they would listen to, trust and obey.

How different God's ways are from ours! The ramifications of the fall are staggering. Think of what it cost God, personally, to allow mankind to become corrupt! Yet God did not fret over Adam and Eve. He did not set up an alarm system, or put barbed wire around the tree of the knowledge of good and evil. There were no warning signs with pictures of the Serpent, no seminars given to learn how to resist him. God simply allowed Adam and Eve to walk away from Him.

➜ Have you ever let someone you love walk away from you? What did it feel like?
It is a painful experience.

➜ What does this tell us about God? What was he willing to lose?
God was willing to lose the love of the ones he had created in his own image, and dearly loved.

We often try to cling to those we love. We manipulate, flatter, coerce, and blackmail people in order to keep them loyal to us. Parents of teenagers do anything they can to keep their kids from open rebellion. We might believe that we are protecting others from harm, but ultimately it is ourselves we are protecting. Rebellion is painful. Open rejection cuts like a knife. Allowing another to walk away can feel like death to everything we ever hoped for.

God was willing to let us go. He let Adam and Eve choose their loyalty. Sometimes we wish God never allowed them the freedom to fall. But in the end it cost God more grief than it ever caused Adam and Eve, or any of their offspring!

MEDITATION

Adam and Eve's ability to obey God's command would not have come from warnings about the Serpent or education about his tactics. Their obedience had to come from their hearts. It is the same with us. We cannot submit from the heart unless we trust his love. What is his love like?

> But Zion said, "The LORD has forsaken me,
> the Lord has forgotten me."
> "Can a mother forget the baby at her breast
> and have no compassion on the child she has borne?
> Though she may forget, I will not forget you!"
> ISAIAH 49:14, 15

This is the love Adam and Eve "forgot." As you meditate on God's love for you this week, pray that you will believe the truth about him, and trust his unfailing love for you.

PRAYER

Father,

You have made me in your image and have always loved me. You never wanted a résumé of performances from me. You want my heart. But I have heaped up my Christian duties and withheld my heart. Please forgive me for pretending to obey you.

You are worthy of my love, my worship, my submission and my trust! Give me the grace to set aside my duties, and draw near to you. The more I know your heart, the more willing I will be to give you mine.

In Jesus' name,
Amen.

But Zion said, "The LORD has forsaken me,
the Lord has forgotten me."
"Can a mother forget the baby at her breast
and have no compassion on the child she has borne?
Though she may forget, I will not forget you!"

ISAIAH 49:14, 15

REFLECT ON THE TEACHING

What is it saying? (Put this verse in your own words.)

WORSHIP

What have I learned that I can praise God for?

REPENTANCE

How do I fail to realize this truth in my life?

What am I like when I forget this truth?
(What do I feel? How do I act? How do I treat God and others?)

THANKFULNESS FOR A SAVIOR

How is Jesus the ultimate example of someone who lived out the truth of this verse?

How is Jesus' death on the cross the ultimate payment for this sin or need of mine?

ASPIRATION

How does this verse show me what I should be or do?

How would I be different if this truth were powerfully real to me? (Ask God for it!)

OBJECTIVE

1. *To realize that obedience is a matter of trust.*

God's command to Adam and Eve appears odd. What does abstaining from one kind of fruit have to do with true obedience? Why didn't God require something more virtuous, like honesty or diligence?

God knows us better than we know ourselves. Moral performance is no indicator of a person's heart. There are motives for morality that have nothing to do with loving God or loving others. Fear is a common source of impeccable behavior. We feel safe when we look like good people. But Jesus does not care about what we look like! He cares about our hearts. And that is exactly the part of ourselves we want to hide.

All it took for Adam and Eve to obey God's command was trust. If Adam and Eve had trusted God's kind intentions toward them, they would have stayed away from the forbidden fruit. But, when they became suspicious of him, they did not hesitate to grab and eat. Adam and Eve were forced to make a choice — trust the God who loved them or defy his command.

Trust is the heart of obedience. If we trust God's heart, we will want to do his will. If we don't, we will defy him. Our hearts are not revealed by our Bible study habits, our church attendance or our many virtues. If we really loved God with all our heart, soul, strength and mind and our neighbor as ourselves, we would be radically changed people. No one would need to tell us how to perform.

The truth is, we don't love God very well, and we love our neighbor even less. We need to face this, so that we can run to our Messiah. But instead of facing the truth about ourselves, we run to moralism or self improvement strategies. It would be like Adam and Eve attending a seminar on obedience, while they were munching on the forbidden fruit.

THEOLOGICAL CONCEPT

Freedom of the Will

Adam and Eve were the only two people who had total freedom to obey or disobey God. All of their descendants are infected with the forbidden fruit's poison. We all have what has been called the "inward curve" of original sin. Each of us is born with the disposition to believe that "God exists for me, people exist for me, and creation exists for me." So, while we make choices and do the things that we want to do, we are not free to not sin.

If you doubt that, just remember what true obedience is. It is loving God with all your heart, soul, strength and mind. Do any of us really do this? The second command is to love your neighbor as yourself. If you wonder who your neighbor is, it is the person you hope God isn't asking you to love like this (Luke 10:29-37).

We are free to choose the ways we will sin, but none of us is free, as Adam and Eve were, to not sin. Most of us love the concept of free will, but get frustrated with God when he lets us make horrific choices that have irrevocable consequences. This is especially true when it comes to Adam and Eve. Their choice to sin became the source of all human misery. We wonder why God ever made it possible for them to destroy the sinless paradise they enjoyed. They did not only destroy their own happiness, they brought pain and suffering upon all their descendants.

Before he created Adam and Eve, God knew that they would choose to listen to his enemy and turn away from him. Jesus had already agreed to go to the cross before Adam and Eve took their first breath (1 Peter 1:20). It is amazing that God would create Adam and Eve and take such delight in them, when he knew what they would do, and what it would cost him to restore their relationship.

God was willing to be vulnerable to his creation. He gave them the gift of choosing whom they would trust and obey. Having the forbidden tree placed in the center of the garden provided Adam and Eve with the gift of exercising their free will. They would either remain loyal to their generous Creator, or despise him by embracing the proud and envious counsel of his enemy. God allowed his image bearers to spurn his love and openly defy him, which they did freely and willfully. He responded by sending his only begotten Son, whom Adam and Eve's offspring despised and rejected. The real mystery is why God loves those who detest his love. As we chose to crucify the holy Son of God, Jesus chose to lay down his life to reconcile us to God. Adam and Eve's free will brought death. God's free will brings eternal life to all who come to his Son.

Several questions arise when we read about the Serpent in the garden. Where did he come from? How did he get into the garden? Why did God allow him there?

Before we consider the answers to these questions, let's take a closer look at his nature. Read the following verses, and list the Serpent's main characteristics in the spaces provided.

> REVELATION 12:9   The great dragon was hurled down — that ancient serpent called the devil, or Satan, who leads the whole world astray. He was hurled to the earth, and his angels with him.
>
> *Satan leads the world astray. He leads people to follow any teaching that keeps them far from Christ.*

> GENESIS 3:1   Now the serpent was more crafty than any of the wild animals the LORD God had made.
>
> *He is crafty or deceptive. He is not what he appears to be, nor do his words reflect his real intentions.*

> JOHN 8:44   You belong to your father, the devil, and you want to carry out your father's desire. He was a murderer from the beginning, not holding to the truth, for there is no truth in him. When he lies, he speaks his native language, for he is a liar and the father of lies. (Jesus was speaking to the Jews who were opposing him.)
>
> *The devil is a murderer and a liar. There is no truth in him. He lies in order to take away life.*

> JOHN 13:2   The evening meal was being served, and the devil had already prompted Judas Iscariot, son of Simon, to betray Jesus.
>
> *The devil leads people to betray others, especially Jesus.*

> EPHESIANS 4:26, 27   "In your anger do not sin": Do not let the sun go down while you are still angry, and do not give the devil a foothold.

→ What might the devil want to do with your anger?
The devil might want to turn your anger into bitterness, causing broken relationships with God and others.

> JAMES 3:14-16   But if you harbor bitter envy and selfish ambition in your hearts,
> do not boast about it or deny the truth. Such "wisdom" does not come down
> from heaven but is earthly, unspiritual, of the devil. For where you have envy and
> selfish ambition, there you find disorder and every evil practice.

→ What sin does the devil call "wise?"
The devil presents bitter envy, selfish ambition and pride as worthy pursuits.

Satan is a brilliant and masterful creature who is full of malice. Look back over the traits that you have listed above. Think about how Satan works to bring division and heartbreak. Murder and betrayal are obvious ways to destroy a relationship. How do the following attitudes or acts ruin marriages, friendships and families?

→ Using words to create a false impression.
Misleading erodes trust.

→ Lying without remorse.
Lying separates close family members and friends by creating suspicion and destroying trust. When someone is unrepentant, there can be no reconciliation or intimacy.

→ Holding onto anger.
When we hold onto anger we build a wall between ourselves and the one who offended us. We become judgmental, proud and bitter. We lose our sense of being a sinner saved by grace. Instead we become self righteous, critical and self centered.

→ Having bitter envy towards another.
When tend to hate those we envy. We believe that we deserve what they have, and conversely, that they do not deserve what they have. We become proud and bitter, angry with God and opposed to his grace.

→ Caring more about your own ambitions than another's well being.
When we put ourselves first, we harm others. We abandon those who deserve our love and end up lonely and empty.

Satan loves to destroy relationships. He, himself, is full of murder, lies, anger, bitter envy and selfish ambition. We learn of his supreme ambition in his third temptation of Jesus. Again, the devil took him to a very high mountain and showed him all the kingdoms of the world and their splendor.

MATTHEW 4:9   "All this I will give you," he said, "if you will bow down and worship me."

➜ What does Satan desire?
Satan desires worship.

➜ Who alone is worthy of worship?
God, alone, is worthy of worship.

➜ Whom does Satan envy?
Satan envies God.

Satan is a dark creature, filled with cruel hatred and unceasing malice. He has another alarming quality. The apostle Paul wrote, "Satan himself masquerades as an angel of light." (2 Corinthians 11:14) It is one thing to face an obvious enemy. But when your enemy comes to you as a compassionate friend, the wound is much deeper. Satan is such an enemy. When he incited Judas to betray Jesus, notice how the betrayal was accomplished.

LUKE 22:47, 48   While he was still speaking a crowd came up, and the man who was called Judas, one of the Twelve, was leading them. He approached Jesus to kiss him, but Jesus asked him, "Judas, are you betraying the Son of Man with a kiss?"

Jesus knows how it feels to be betrayed by a close friend. He also knows the one who is behind it. Judas was not the first person that Satan enticed to betray God. Have you ever wondered why the devil went after Adam and Eve?

➜ How might tempting them to sin against God gratify Satan's malicious desires?
Satan would be gratified to know that he had destroyed the loving relationship that God had with Adam and Eve.

We do not know why God allowed Satan to come into the Garden. Surely God could have prevented his presence and thus prevented the fall. He chose not to. The Bible does not tell us why. But God did limit Satan's power. When we look at the actual temptation of Eve, we will discover that the Serpent's influence was limited to words. God simply permitted Adam and Eve to hear another voice and decide what to do with it.

MEDITATION

Adam and Eve lived in Paradise where they could walk with God and hear his voice. In a setting that sang of God's goodness and glory, a serpent appeared and spoke lies. Now we live in a fallen world full of danger, deception and death. The Son of God came into our fallen world spoke only the truth.

> *The thief comes only to steal and kill and destroy;*
> *I have come that they may have life, and have it to the full.*
> JOHN 10:10

Satan is real. He wants to destroy us. His primary desire is to alienate us from God and each other. Jesus is also real, and more powerful than Satan. He came to heal us. His compassionate desire is to reconcile us to God and each other. He calls us to find our life in him, and have it to the full!

PRAYER

Father,

The Serpent is an evil enemy. He hates you, he hates me and he hates everybody I love. When I listen to him I end up alienated from you and isolated. He is a thief who steals my joy and my peace.

Expose the lies I have listened to and embraced. Show me the difference between the truth and the Serpent's deceptions. Give me the grace to repent for listening to him. Set me free from his designs so I can draw near to you and receive the life you long to give me.

In Jesus' name,
Amen.

The thief comes only to steal and kill and destroy;
I have come that they may have life, and have it to the full.

JOHN 10:10

REFLECT ON THE TEACHING

What is it saying? (Put this verse in your own words.)

WORSHIP

What have I learned that I can praise God for?

REPENTANCE

How do I fail to realize this truth in my life?

What am I like when I forget this truth?
(What do I feel? How do I act? How do I treat God and others?)

Thankfulness for a Savior

How is Jesus the ultimate example of someone who lived out the truth of this verse?

How is Jesus' death on the cross the ultimate payment for this sin or need of mine?

Aspiration

How does this verse show me what I should be or do?

How would I be different if this truth were powerfully real to me? (Ask God for it!)

OBJECTIVES

1. *Dependence verses Independence.*

The goal of man-made religion is independent perfection. Notice what the Serpent offered Eve. She would be like God and be wise. Is there anything wrong with being a wise and godly woman? Imagine that someone offered you an experience that would make you just like Jesus — as loving, as wise, as obedient. The magic wand would wave over you and voila: wise, like God! Would you be tempted? This is the temptation Eve faced. Being like God without needing God.

The goal of Christianity is NOT independent perfection. It is the perfection of our dependence. We do need God! We cannot take a single breath without him. Yet, we hate being needy. We wish we could take control of our lives completely. This is what Eve came to desire. She did not envision becoming an evil deity. Instead she envisioned being wise in her own strength. She would not have to depend on the God who was suddenly looking more like a threat than a blessing.

Encourage your group to consider why they want to be better people than they are. The truth is that Satan has deceived us more than we know. We love earning our own glory more than we love the joy of intimate dependence on Christ.

To bring this home, ask those in your group to remember a time when their work was going to be noticed. The task can be anything from having people over to dinner to making a presentation before a large group of people. Were they anxious? Was their time and energy spent on seeking God and relying upon him, or on working to ensure an acceptable performance? Whose glory were they pursuing? If we are honest, we will admit that we are just like Eve, craving our own glory and eating forbidden fruit to achieve it. That is why we need a Savior.

Dependence upon Christ is only sweet when Christ, himself, is sweet to us. The Apostle Paul loved depending upon Jesus. He continually faced situations that were way too hard for him to handle. Yet, in all his troubles, he experienced God's compassionate presence. He learned the beauty of relying on God, who can raise the dead, instead of relying on his own wisdom and virtue. Read the first chapter of 2 Corinthians to see the beauty of dependence that Paul enjoyed.

THEOLOGICAL CONCEPT

Idolatry

An idol is anything that we turn to apart from God, or in addition to God, to satisfy the deep thirst in our soul. When we do not trust God, we always run to an idol. The Heidelberg Catechism vividly describes genuine love for God and the sin of idolatry.

Question 94
Question 94: What does God enjoin in the first commandment?
Answer 94: That I, as sincerely as I desire the salvation of my own soul, avoid and flee from all idolatry, sorcery, soothsaying, superstition, invocation of saints, or any other creatures; and learn

rightly to know the only true God; trust in him alone, with humility and patience submit to him; expect all good things from him only; love, fear, and glorify him with my whole heart; so that I renounce and forsake all creatures, rather than commit even the least thing contrary to his will.

Question 95

Question 95: What is idolatry?

Answer 95: Idolatry is, instead of, or besides that one true God, who has manifested himself in his word, to contrive, or have any other object, in which men place their trust.

Answer 94 is simply a description of what it means to truly trust God. It helps us understand why we need to know that God is good. We cannot submit and expect all good things from him unless we know he is the only source of "living water" for our souls. It is our unbelief, as unjustified as Eve's, that leads us to idolatry.

We will never be completely free from idolatry until we see Jesus face to face. We always believe that someone or something besides God will give us what we really need. But idolatry makes us a slave to things that can never satisfy our deepest need. If we look for life in achievement or in gaining the approval of others we will die of thirst. Our hard labor will wear us out and leave us empty. But if we trust in Christ and learn to know him intimately our souls will be renewed and Jesus, himself, will fill us to overflowing (John 4:13,14).

The Serpent came into the Garden. He did not overwhelm Eve as a superior spiritual being, but came as a snake. He was a creature under her dominion. He did not use any hidden power, but tempted her with simple words.

As we study Satan's conversation with Eve, we have to look beneath the surface. We have learned that the Serpent was a subtle liar. He was not what he appeared to be, nor did his words mean what they appeared to mean. In order to see what he was trying to accomplish, we have to think carefully about the words he chose and the impression they created.

> GENESIS 3:1   Now the serpent was more crafty than any of the wild animals the LORD God had made. He said to the woman, "Did God really say, 'You must not eat from any tree in the garden'?"

The Serpent knew what God had prohibited. He was not questioning Eve to learn the truth but to take it from her. Let's see how his questions achieved his purpose.

➜ From how many trees did God say that Adam and Eve could not eat?
One.

➜ From how many trees did the Serpent suggest that God had forbidden them to eat?
Satan suggested that God had forbidden them to eat the fruit from every tree in the garden.

➜ What kind of God would create a garden full of beautiful trees, loaded with delicious fruit and say, "You can't have any!"?
Answers will vary. God would be at best withholding and at worst sadistic.

The Serpent wanted to create a view of God that had no basis in fact. Without providing any evidence, Satan planted a seed of suspicion in Eve's mind and put her on the defensive.

➜ In view of her relationship with God, how should Eve have responded?
Eve should have told the Serpent that his suggestion was ridiculous. She could have used the opportunity to show all the free gifts God had given her. Better yet, she should have run to God.

GENESIS 3:2, 3   The woman said to the serpent, "We may eat fruit from the trees in the garden, but God did say, 'You must not eat fruit from the tree that is in the middle of the garden, and you must not touch it, or you will die.' "

Think of a person who has meant more to you than anyone else in your life.

➜ What is it about him or her that you love and admire?
Answers will vary.

➜ How would you reply to someone who suggested that this person is selfish and cruel?
Usually there would be anger and a desire to set the record straight.

➜ What is missing from Eve's answer?
Eve did not defend God's goodness and generosity. She did not seem offended at all.

On the surface, Eve's reply looks honest enough. But there is something about her response that indicates that she was "listening" to the serpent, taking his impression to heart.

➜ What did Eve add to God's actual command concerning the tree of the knowledge of good and evil?
Eve added that she could not touch the tree.

➜ What impression of God did Eve create by adding these words to his command?
  Eve made God appear stricter than he actually was.

The Serpent was now ready to attack God's character directly. He had succeeded in raising doubts about God's love. Next he told Eve outright lies.

> GENESIS 3:4, 5   "You will not surely die," the serpent said to the woman. "For God knows that when you eat of it your eyes will be opened, and you will be like God, knowing good and evil."

➜ According to Satan, what was God's motive for prohibiting Eve to eat from the tree of the knowledge of good and evil?
  God did not want Eve's eyes to be opened. He did not want her to be like God, knowing good and evil.

What kind of God would:

➜ tell Eve that she would die when he knew that she would actually become a greater person? (Satan's lie.)
  Answers will vary. At best God would be keeping Eve from greatness, at worst God would be jealously keeping Eve under his domination.

➜ want to keep Eve's eyes closed?
  God would be oppressive and controlling.

➜ be afraid that Eve might become as great as he is?
  God would be insecure and more devoted to his status than her well being.

→ If God were like this, would you trust and obey him, or would you turn away to gain a better life for yourself?
I would turn away from him to find a better life elsewhere.

Let's look at what Satan appeared to be offering Eve.

→ What did Satan say that Eve would become if she ate the forbidden fruit?
She would become like God.

→ According to the Serpent, who cared more about Eve, God or himself?
The Serpent seemed to be trying to help Eve escape from an unfair God.

→ Whose interests did the Serpent entice Eve to put first?
The Serpent enticed Eve to care about herself above anyone else.

→ How could Eve achieve what was "best" for her?
Eve had to eat the forbidden fruit.

Eve was at a critical juncture. Let's look at how she made her choice.

> GENESIS 3:6   When the woman saw that the fruit of the tree was good for food and pleasing to the eye, and also desirable for gaining wisdom, she took some and ate it. She also gave some to her husband, who was with her, and he ate it.

→ Where did Eve focus her attention?
Eve focused on the forbidden fruit.

According to Genesis 2:9, every tree in the garden was as beautiful and as good for food as this tree.

→ What unique gift did Eve think she could acquire from the forbidden tree?
Eve thought she could acquire wisdom.

→ Is there anything wrong with desiring wisdom?
True wisdom is a good thing to desire.

→ What was wrong with Eve's desire?
Eve was grasping an independent wisdom that would make her equal to God. She was willing to disobey God in order to become like him.

→ What did Eve do?
She took some of the forbidden fruit and ate it. She also gave some to Adam who was with her.

→ Did Eve get what she desired?
No!

One of Satan's most deceptive tactics is to present us with good things and tempt us to grasp them as the ultimate thing. Wanting to be Christ-like and wise is not bad in and of itself. But when striving to be like Jesus feels more important than coming to him as we are, the Serpent has deceived us.

Our view of God is the single most important factor in our obedience. If we think God is withholding his best, then like Eve, we will turn away from him and seek life somewhere else. Thankfully, God is not like Satan's awful caricatures. He loves us dearly and has our best interests in mind.

MEDITATION

Satan never delivers what he promises. He deals in deception and broken dreams. He promises living water to our souls, but only delivers dust. God is trustworthy. He alone gives us what we really need.

> My people have committed two sins: they have forsaken me, the spring of living water, and have dug their own cisterns, broken cisterns that cannot hold water.
>
> JEREMIAH 2:13

> If anyone is thirsty, let him come to me and drink. Whoever believes in me, as the Scripture has said, streams of living water will flow from within him.
>
> JOHN 7:37, 38

PRAYER

Father,

You have never withheld your heart from me or deceived me in any way. But I have believed outlandish lies about you and run to my own ambitions to fill my empty soul. I have not found any relief from my thirst.

I deserve to remain empty. But you love me. You sent Jesus to bring me back to you. If I come, you promise that streams of living water will flow from within me. Help me to see the ways I have run from you to find life. But more than that, give me the grace to forsake my broken cisterns and return to you. I want your living water!

In the name of Jesus,
Amen.

If anyone is thirsty, let him come to me and drink.
Whoever believes in me, as the Scripture has said,
streams of living water will flow from within him.

JOHN 7:37, 38

REFLECT ON THE TEACHING

What is it saying? (Put this verse in your own words.)

WORSHIP

What have I learned that I can praise God for?

REPENTANCE

How do I fail to realize this truth in my life?

What am I like when I forget this truth?
(What do I feel? How do I act? How do I treat God and others?)

Thankfulness for a Savior

How is Jesus the ultimate example of someone who lived out the truth of this verse?

How is Jesus' death on the cross the ultimate payment for this sin or need of mine?

Aspiration

How does this verse show me what I should be or do?

How would I be different if this truth were powerfully real to me? (Ask God for it!)

OBJECTIVE

1. *To welcome God's conviction.*

The apostle John was close to Jesus. He called himself "the apostle that Jesus loved" (John 13:23, 21:7, 20). When he chose the words that best describe Jesus, he wrote: "The Word became flesh and made his dwelling among us. We have seen his glory, the glory of the One and Only, who came from the Father, full of grace and truth" (John 1:14).

John saw Jesus speak the truth boldly, when most would remain silent. But Jesus always spoke with a gracious purpose. John also wrote: "For the law was given through Moses; grace and truth came through Jesus Christ" (John 1:17). The Law brings condemnation because we are law breakers. But Jesus brings grace and truth. Grace comes first, then comes truth. This is what God is like.

Jesus' questions were always designed to bring men from self-deception to honesty. He often asked the Pharisees specific questions to expose their hypocrisy (Matthew 21:23-27; Luke 6:6-11; Luke10:29, 36; Luke 13:10-17; Luke 14:1-6). He was not sarcastic or mean- spirited. Instead, he gave others an opportunity to see themselves for what they really were. But they resented the exposure and became determined to silence him permanently. They preferred to remain in the dark.

Jesus also used questions to lead his followers into deeper faith (Matthew 6:26-30; Matthew 7:9-11; Matthew 16:5-12; Luke 8:22-25; John 11:25,40). His disciples knew his heart, and even though they constantly struggled, they let his words change them. They were slow to comprehend Jesus, just like we are. But Jesus never lost patience with them, and he will remain patient with us as well.

We all know the voice of accusation and condemnation. It is never the voice of God. Satan is the Accuser, not God! God is "compassionate and gracious, slow to anger and abounding in love" (Psalm 103:8).

In Genesis 3 we see how God approached Adam and Eve after they had disobeyed him. He came in the cool of the day, taking the humble form of a man. He allowed Adam and Eve to hide themselves among the trees he had made. God had the power to terrify and completely expose them. But he loved them. He did not want to humiliate them or prove how they deserved his fury. He never resorted to interrogation tactics to force them to confess. Notice carefully how his questions were designed for their benefit, not their harm. God gave them an opportunity to admit the truth before they were specifically asked. He allowed them to speak from their hearts. And that is exactly what they did. Their answers were more self incriminating than anything God could have forced from them.

God only works to reveal to us the sin that he intends to pardon and redeem. When we stay in denial, we ruin our lives and the lives of those we love. Jesus longs for us to respond to his questions and admit the truth. He will never abandon us. Instead he will hold us and walk with us through the toughest realizations. He knows how painful it is for us to learn the truth about ourselves. But he also knows the freedom and joy that come with genuine confession, repentance and forgiveness. Psalm 32 illustrates both the pain of denial and the joy of welcoming God's healing conviction.

2. *To repent of blame-shifting.*

Adam and Eve responded to God's questions by shifting their blame to others. God did not allow such a transfer of guilt. He won't allow it with us either. Yet God is wise. He sympathizes with our weakness (Hebrews 4:15). For example, he knows that abuse leaves its mark, especially in childhood. The shame and the intense fears that develop are fully comprehended by our compassionate Savior. Abuse distorts our sense of guilt and shame and confuses our conscience. That is why Jesus counsels us to come to him for "eye salve" so that we can begin to see clearly (Revelation 3:18).

Nevertheless, our real sin is always our own fault. When we lie, we are culpable. When we gossip, we are to blame. We can either cling to our imagined innocence, or we can confess our sin. It is painful to face the truth about ourselves. We cannot do it if we are putting our hope in our own innate goodness. Like Adam and Eve, we will have to find someone to blame for what we have done. However, when we remember the cross we can let go of our need to be innocent. We have access to a throne of grace. Adam and Eve had the opportunity to run to God, who still loved them. They chose instead to shift the blame and harden their hearts. They were the losers. We also lose when we choose to blame others for our own thoughts, words or deeds.

Adam did not only blame Eve for his sin. He also blamed God. He inferred that God was the real culprit, since he was the one who created Eve. Blaming God for our sin is another way we avoid the truth. Job did this when his suffering mounted and felt unjustifiable. God responded with questions. "Would you discredit my justice? Would you condemn me to justify yourself?" (Job 40:8).

If God were to ask us these questions, we would have to answer, "yes!" We blame God for making us sinful, for giving us sinful people to deal with, for creating situations too difficult to handle. But, once again, we are only deceiving ourselves. Just like Adam, we do not want to be admit our sin and our need for a Savior. We want to be viewed as people who are handling, with admirable endurance, the adversities that God has dished out. We feel like God should be asking our forgiveness for making life too hard.

Life is hard and people can be callous, cruel and oppressive. It would be unreasonable for God to demand sinless perfection from sinners. But God has never demanded this from Adam's descendents. Instead he has demanded repentance (admitting the truth about who we really are) and faith in a Savior who died to pay the full penalty for our sin.

God has not required us to perform, but to believe in his Son. Only sinners want a Savior. Our blame-shifting makes us hostile to Jesus. Like Adam, we lie to ourselves and harden our heart against the lover of our souls. But if we let God show us our true sin, we will find Jesus intensely valuable. We will glory in the cross like Paul did (Galatians 6:14) and let life's painful struggles lead us to depend upon Jesus in deeper ways (2 Corinthians 1:9).

THEOLOGICAL CONCEPT

Original Sin

As soon as they ate the forbidden fruit, Adam and Eve changed dramatically. In a moment, fear replaced love, hiding replaced intimacy, and false accusation replaced honesty. Every child of theirs is infected with the poison of the forbidden fruit. Theologians have called our inherited fallen nature, 'original sin.'

The Heidelberg catechism draws the striking contrast between what God requires (what Adam and Eve were like before they disobeyed) and what we have become.

Question 4
Question 4: What does the law of God require of us?
Answer 4: Christ teaches us that briefly, Matt. 22:37-40, "Thou shalt love the Lord thy God with all thy heart, with all thy soul, and with all thy mind, and with all thy strength. This is the first and the great commandment; and the second is like unto it, Thou shalt love thy neighbour as thyself. On these two commandments hang all the law and the prophets."

Question 5
Question 5: Canst thou keep all these things perfectly?
Answer 5: In no wise; for I am prone by nature to hate God and my neighbour.

We are the opposite of what we ought to be. We ought to love the God who created and redeemed us. Instead, we are naturally suspicious of him and angry when he opposes our agenda. We ought to love our neighbor. But we hate those who bring us more trouble than help.

There is something deeply wrong with each of us. Paul called it our "flesh" (sinful nature) and explained that all kinds of behaviors spring forth from this inner corruption.

"The acts of the sinful nature are obvious: sexual immorality, impurity and debauchery; idolatry and witchcraft; hatred, discord, jealousy, fits of rage, selfish ambition, dissensions, factions and envy; drunkenness, orgies, and the like. I warn you, as I did before, that those who live like this will not inherit the kingdom of God" (Galatians 5:19-21).

Notice that Paul includes the sins of moral as well as immoral people. Moralists are notoriously proud, selfishly ambitious, and full of hatred and discord. When we are "right" we are only too ready to break away from the "wrong" group of people with their "wrong" beliefs and behaviors. This is as much a fruit of original sin as sexual immorality and drunkenness.

Our sinful nature also affects our ability to reason. Paul says that "the mind of our flesh" is hostile to God and unable to submit to him (Romans 8:7). Our reasoning is darkened by our sinful bent to suppress the truth about God and to follow any other "god" that will fit better with our selfish desires and ambitions (Romans 1:21-25). Paul described our minds as "deceived," our will as "enslaved," and our affections as "malicious."

"At one time we too were foolish, disobedient, deceived and enslaved by all kinds of passions and pleasures. We lived in malice and envy, being hated and hating one another" (Titus 3:3).

All of us are like this by nature. We are expert hiders. Think of the energy we expend trying to look like better people than we are. We truly are Adam and Eve's offspring — full of shame and hiding behind the fig leaves of pretense.

Our sin cannot be "cured" or overcome by will power, education, or even human love. God's Spirit alone can overcome our sin nature. When Nicodemus, a relatively good man, came to Jesus, the first thing Jesus said was, "I tell you the truth, no one can see the Kingdom of God unless he is born again." Nicodemus, like everyone else, had to be reborn, not improved. The Spirit of God must come into our hearts and renew our minds (Ephesians 4:23). He, alone, enables us to stop living for the corrupt desires of our flesh (Romans 8:7).

Original sin is unconquerable apart from the cross. We cannot teach ourselves to love God or our neighbor. By God's grace, we are not as bad as we could be. But we are corrupt in every part of our being — our minds, our wills, and our affections. We need a rescue.

Y̶ou may have noticed that Adam was with Eve when she ate the fruit. We do not know why Adam stood by silently and let Eve eat from the forbidden tree. Later God said to Adam, "Because you listened to your wife..." Did Adam listen to Eve the same way that Eve listened to the Serpent? All we know for sure is that Adam also disobeyed and ate the forbidden fruit.

How did Adam and Eve change? Did they become like God? Were they full of wisdom? Sadly, the opposite was true.

> **GENESIS 2:25**   The man and his wife were both naked, and they felt no shame.

> **GENESIS 3:7**   Then the eyes of both of them were opened, and they realized they were naked; so they sewed fig leaves together and made coverings for themselves.

➜ How did Adam and Eve feel about being naked before they disobeyed?
They were unashamed.

➜ How did they feel about it after the Fall?
They were uncomfortable and wanted to hide from each other.

➜ Why do you think they felt the need to cover themselves?
Answers may vary. They were afraid of the other's gaze and felt ashamed of what was in their own heart.

It is hard to imagine what Adam and Eve's sudden transformation felt like. It must have been a shock to feel selfish desires replacing the love they had always known. Fear became their ruling emotion as they looked at each other. But that was nothing compared to their fear of facing God.

> **GENESIS 3:8**   Then the man and his wife heard the sound of the LORD God as he was walking in the garden in the cool of the day, and they hid from the LORD God among the trees of the garden.

When God came, fig leaves were not enough of a covering.

→ What did they do when they heard the sound of his footsteps?
They hid from the Lord.

→ What had become mankind's instinctive reaction to God's presence?
We want to hide from God.

When Adam and Eve spoke their new nature was revealed.

> GENESIS 3:9-13   But the LORD God called to the man, "Where are you?" He
> answered, "I heard you in the garden, and I was afraid because I was naked; so I
> hid." And he said, "Who told you that you were naked? Have you eaten from the
> tree that I commanded you not to eat from?" The man said, "The woman you
> put here with me — she gave me some fruit from the tree, and I ate it." Then the
> LORD God said to the woman, "What is this you have done?" The woman said,
> "The serpent deceived me, and I ate."

God did not thunder accusations at Adam and Eve from heaven. He did not drag them from their hiding places. Instead, he walked to them in the garden, in the non-threatening form of a man, and asked them questions.

God and Satan both approached Adam and Eve with questions. But their motives were completely opposite.

→ What was Satan trying to do when he asked his question?
Satan was trying to cover up the truth.

→ What was God trying to do when he asked Adam and Eve his questions?
God was trying to uncover the truth.

Questions can create deception or help us discover the truth.

➜ Do you know someone who asks the kind of questions that help you understand your own thoughts? How valuable is this relationship?
This kind of relationship is very valuable.

➜ If you trust this person, how will you respond to his or her probing questions?
I will be as honest as I can.

Look at Adam's answer to God's first question.

➜ How much was Adam revealing to God?
Adam was revealing his fear, but not his sin.

➜ What did Adam neglect to mention?
He neglected to mention that he had eaten the forbidden fruit.

Next, God asked a "yes" or "no" question. But Adam said neither.

➜ Who did Adam blame for his sin?
Eve.

➜ If God had immediately carried out the consequence for eating the forbidden fruit, what would have happened to Eve?
Eve would have died.

→ Who was Adam trying to protect?
Himself.

→ Who was Adam willing to harm?
Eve.

Adam also blamed someone else for his sin. He blamed the one who put Eve in the garden.

→ Who was Adam ultimately blaming for his sin?
God.

Blaming God for our own sin is a common way that we hide the truth from ourselves. We end up the losers when we refuse to admit who we are and what we have done. God and others are kept far away, and we end up living a lie.

→ Do you see any sign of remorse or repentance in Adam?
No. Adam only showed self-centered fear.

God turned to Eve next.

→ Who did Eve blame for her sin?
The Serpent.

→ How did Eve hide her true motive for eating the fruit?
Eve did not tell God that she wanted to become like him and had deliberately disobeyed. She merely mentioned that she had been deceived. She was not deceived into believing that she would be obeying God by eating the forbidden fruit. Instead she was only deceived about the outcome of her deliberate disobedience.

➔ Does she show any signs of remorse or repentance?
   No.

Adam and Eve were given the opportunity to admit what they had done, and what they had become. But they resisted God's probing questions and shifted the blame for their own sin. God was not fooled by their answers. It is likely he was deeply grieved. God still loved Adam and Eve, but they seem to have lost all love for him.

We are Adam and Eve's offspring. We also resist God's probing questions and shift blame when we are exposed.

The only sin that keeps us from Jesus is our refusal to face the truth about ourselves. If you read through the Gospels (Matthew, Mark, Luke and John) you will discover that obvious "sinners" were always quicker to put their trust in Jesus than the religious leaders. Jesus explained why.

> MARK 2:17   On hearing this, Jesus said to them, "It is not the healthy who need a doctor, but the sick. I have not come to call the righteous, but sinners."

➔ Who did Jesus come for?
   Jesus came for those who are sick and sinful.

➔ Who did Jesus NOT come for?
   Jesus did not come for those who are healthy and righteous.

When Jesus asks questions in Scripture, he is not trying to shame or harm us. He is helping us to see our need for a Savior. Ultimately Jesus wants to give us something much better than our sin. He wants to give us himself. When we resist him, we are locking our heart's door against the only doctor who can heal us.

MEDITATION

When we harden our hearts against God, we lose out on his greatest gift — complete forgiveness and healing.

> *Praise the LORD, O my soul,*
> *and forget not all his benefits —*
> *who forgives all your sins*
> *and heals all your diseases.*
> PSALM 103:2, 3

As you ponder these verses, pray for the grace to believe that it is better to be forgiven and healed than to be "right."

PRAYER

Father,

It is hard to look at Adam and Eve. They changed so drastically! When you came to them they hid. When you asked them what happened, they lied. I am like them. I hide from you in fear. I resist accepting the blame for my own sin.

But you sent your Son for sinners like me. You love me so much! I need your searching questions so I can learn the truth. As I meditate on your promises this week, give me the grace to believe that you only expose my sin in order to forgive me and bring healing into my life. Don't let me hide from you.

In Jesus' name,
Amen.

Praise the LORD, O my soul,
and forget not all his benefits —
who forgives all your sins
and heals all your diseases.

Psalm 103:2, 3

REFLECT ON THE TEACHING

What is it saying? (Put this verse in your own words.)

WORSHIP

What have I learned that I can praise God for?

REPENTANCE

How do I fail to realize this truth in my life?

What am I like when I forget this truth?
(What do I feel? How do I act? How do I treat God and others?)

THANKFULNESS FOR A SAVIOR

How is Jesus the ultimate example of someone who lived out the truth of this verse?

How is Jesus' death on the cross the ultimate payment for this sin or need of mine?

ASPIRATION

How does this verse show me what I should be or do?

How would I be different if this truth were powerfully real to me? (Ask God for it!)

PART TWO �֍ THE RESCUE

OBJECTIVES

1. *To understand the nature of eternal life.*

   When the Bible speaks of eternal life, it is not referring to unending existence. Jesus explained what eternal life really is. "Now this is eternal life: that they may know you, the only true God, and Jesus Christ, whom you have sent" (John 17:3).

   Eternal life is knowing God. It is having his Spirit in our hearts and living in a close relationship with Jesus. Only a restored relationship with God brings eternal life.

   In banishing us from Eden, God was not refusing us eternal life. He was preserving us from an eternal existence as sinners in alienation from him. God was not willing to give us up. But eternal life would not come from the tree of life. It would come from the cross. God knew the cost of giving us eternal life and he was willing to pay it. Jesus would die for the sin of eating the forbidden fruit as well as every sin that flows from our self centered hearts. Those who hear the message and believe receive the eternal life that Jesus earned for them.

2. *To realize that Jesus alone is the solution for the fall.*

   God's solution for the fall is Jesus. The seed of the woman is the only one to crush the head of the Serpent and redeem a fallen humanity. God does not offer any additional solutions or training programs. There is no other way to earn our way back into God's favor, or to keep it. When we looked at original sin we saw that our hearts are not fixable. All we can do is rearrange the ways we hide, or cover our shame. For example, achievement is a powerful "fig leaf." If we do something truly great, we hope it will cover all our shame and insecurities. But achievement cannot get inside our hearts. We are still the same empty people whether or not we turn in a wonderful performance or accomplish something great.

   It may look like God provided another way to earn his favor when he gave the Law. But the apostle Paul explained that salvation has always been a matter of grace, not moral achievement (Galatians 3:15-19). God spoke to the Serpent about the seed who would come (Genesis 3:15). Later he gave a promise to Abraham concerning his offspring, the seed through whom all the nations of the earth will be blessed (Genesis 22:18). The law, which came much later, did not nullify God's promise and create a new way to earn God's favor. Instead, the law showed us God's holiness, exposed us as hopeless sinners, and prepared us to trust in the "seed" who was coming.

   Paul made it clear throughout his epistles that merit and grace are opposites. After the fall, God made a promise about a coming Messiah. Our hope is in him, or it is misplaced. Salvation is through promise and only those who continually put their faith in the "seed" receive all that Jesus has earned for them.

Theological concept

The Bible is about Jesus.

I've asked several groups of people, from teens to adults, who the Bible is primarily about. Without exception, the majority believed that the Bible is primarily about us, and what we need to do to be saved. It may come as a surprise to discover that the Bible is not primarily about us, but about Jesus. Jesus, himself, said that the Bible is all about him. Like us, the people in Jesus' time thought the Bible was about learning and keeping God's commands. Jesus said this to them: "You diligently study the Scriptures because you think that by them you possess eternal life. These are the Scriptures that testify about me, yet you refuse to come to me to have life" (John 5: 39,40).

Jesus told the Jews that the Scriptures they so diligently studied were about him. They were written to lead them to the Messiah. Jesus wants us to study the Bible according to its design. It is designed to make you come to Jesus for eternal life.

We are so resistant to this idea. We instinctively believe that we must do something to merit eternal life. Even Jesus' disciples believed this. He repeatedly told them about his coming death and resurrection. But they did not see the need for the cross. Like us, they believed that they only needed a teacher to help them understand God and what he requires. They did not comprehend their need for a Savior who would die in their place.

We are saved by grace through faith in Christ alone, and not by the works of the law. As Paul said, if righteousness could have come through keeping the law, God would never have sent his Son to die (Galatians 3:21,22). But God did send his Son! He sent him for us because we need a Savior, not an advisor, not a helper.

After Jesus died, his followers felt hopeless. As two disciples made their way to Emmaus, Jesus appeared to them without revealing his identity. When he asked why they were downcast, they told him about the death of Jesus. Then they explained, "We had hoped that he was the one who was going to redeem Israel." These men could not conceive of a crucified Messiah. Like all of mankind, they had misunderstood the Scriptures. Jesus corrected them, using every portion of the Old Testament to reveal how it all pointed to him.

He said to them, "How foolish you are, and how slow of heart to believe all that the prophets have spoken! Did not the Christ have to suffer these things and then enter his glory?" And beginning with Moses and all the Prophets, he explained to them what was said in all the Scriptures concerning himself (Luke 24:25-27).

The disciples were amazed by his words and urged him to stay with them. Jesus complied long enough to break bread with them. Then their eyes were opened to recognize who he was. At that moment he disappeared from their sight. They asked each other, "Were not our hearts burning within us while he talked with us on the road and opened the Scriptures to us?" (verse 32).

Let the paradigm shift that Jesus gave his followers sink in. The Bible is about him. May this truth cause your heart to burn within you as well.

Charles D. Drew wrote an excellent book on this subject entitled, THE ANCIENT LOVE SONG. If you are interested in further study on the centrality of Christ in the Scriptures, this book is easy to read and quite helpful.

Adam and Eve were no longer what they had been at Creation. In one act of disobedience they became more like the Serpent than the God who created them. How would God restore Adam and Eve, and their sinful offspring? Could he undo what was done? No. Did God have a better plan? Yes! First, let's look at what was not in God's plan.

> GENESIS 3:22-24   And the LORD God said, "The man has now become like one of us, knowing good and evil. He must not be allowed to reach out his hand and take also from the tree of life and eat, and live forever." So the LORD God banished him from the Garden of Eden to work the ground from which he had been taken. After he drove the man out, he placed on the east side of the Garden of Eden cherubim and a flaming sword flashing back and forth to guard the way to the tree of life.

At first glance these verses seem confusing.

➔ Did Adam and Eve actually acquire a knowledge of good and evil that resembled God's?
   No. They became less like God..

Dr. Timothy Keller gives an analogy that helps us to understand the kind of "knowing" that Adam and Eve obtained. He compares what they got to the Bubonic plague. There are two ways to learn about the Bubonic plague. You can study it in order to protect yourself and help others. Or you can catch it and die from it. Adam and Eve chose the latter. They got what they wanted, but instead of it being a dream come true, it turned out to be a nightmare. Adam and Eve became corrupt. They "caught" sin and were slowly dying from it.

➔ What reason did God give for banishing Adam and Eve from the garden?
   Adam must not be allowed to eat from the tree of life and live forever.

➔ What might eternal life look like for sinful people in a fallen world?
   It would be a life of eternal sin and separation from God.

Living forever is not the same thing as eternal life.

> JOHN 17:3   Now this is eternal life: that they may know you, the only true God, and Jesus Christ, whom you have sent.

→ What is the eternal life that God wants us to have?
Eternal life is knowing the only true God and his Son, Jesus Christ.

God did not plan for mankind to live forever in alienation from him. He planned something much better.

→ How did God guard the tree of life?
God sent cherubim (angels) and a flaming sword which flashed back and forth to guard the way to the tree of life.

Eternal life would not come from the tree of life. It would come from another source. God gave the first hint of his plan when he condemned the Serpent.

> GENESIS 3:15   And I will put enmity between you and the woman, and between your offspring and hers; he will crush your head, and you will strike his heel.

This verse begins by describing the hatred that would exist between the people who belong to the Serpent and those who belong to the woman. But the second half of this verse talks about a conflict between the Serpent, himself, and a single offspring of the woman.

→ What will the Serpent do to the offspring of the woman?
He will strike his heel.

→ What will the woman's offspring do to the Serpent?
He will crush the Serpent's head.

→ Who comes out the winner?
The offspring of the woman.

→ Do you know who this offspring is?
Jesus!

GALATIANS 4:4, 5   But when the time had fully come, God sent his Son, born of a woman, born under law, to redeem those under law, that we might receive the full rights of sons.

HEBREWS 2:14, 15   Since the children have flesh and blood, he too shared in their humanity so that by his death he might destroy him who holds the power of death -- that is, the devil -- and free those who all their lives were held in slavery by their fear of death

➜ Who is the woman's offspring?
Jesus Christ, the Son of God.

➜ According to these verses, how many people take part in destroying the Serpent and rescuing mankind from death?
Only One.

It is critical for us to know that our rescue comes from God, alone. We cannot perform ourselves back into the Garden of Eden. We can modify our behavior, but we cannot make our hearts clean. The entire Bible, from Genesis 3:15 on, is about this child to come -- Jesus our Redeemer.

The Pharisees thought the Scriptures were about achieving a level of obedience that the LORD would reward with eternal life. But this was not Jesus' understanding of the Bible.

JOHN 5:39, 40   You diligently study the Scriptures because you think that by them you possess eternal life. These are the Scriptures that testify about me, yet you refuse to come to me to have life.

JOHN 5:46   If you believed Moses, you would believe me, for he wrote about me.

LUKE 24:25-27   He said to them, "How foolish you are, and how slow of heart to believe all that the prophets have spoken! Did not the Christ have to suffer these things and then enter his glory?" And beginning with Moses and all the Prophets, he explained to them what was said in all the Scriptures concerning himself.

LUKE 24:44   He said to them, "This is what I told you while I was still with you: Everything must be fulfilled that is written about me in the Law of Moses, the Prophets and the Psalms."

➜ According to Jesus, who is the Old Testament primarily about?
The Old Testament is about Jesus.

Ultimately there are only two ways to approach God. The first way is to try to rescue yourself by working hard to become good enough to meet God's approval. The Pharisees chose this way and rejected the child. The second way is to trust the child who came to crush the Serpent's head. It is to reject your own attempts at self-improvement and come to the One whom God appointed long ago to rescue you.

It is liberating to realize that the Bible is about Jesus. We do not have to rescue ourselves or anyone else. This child alone is God's remedy for the fall.

MEDITATION

Jesus came because he has compassion on you. He knows the fears you feel deep inside, and how they lead you to a slavish drive to perform. He did not come to condemn you, but to rescue you.

> *Since the children have flesh and blood,*
> *he too shared in their humanity so that by his death*
> *he might destroy him who holds the power of death — that is, the devil —*
> *and free those who all their lives were held in slavery*
> *by their fear of death.*
>
> HEBREWS 2:14, 15

PRAYER

Father,

We are humbled again by your tender love for us. We find it so hard to face our deep need for a total rescue. Instead, we believe that we can fix ourselves. You know the truth about us. You gave us what we need, a Savior. You see our slavery to fear, and the inevitability of death. You sent Jesus to die, so that we can live without fear.

Adam and Eve knew your love because of your gift of creation. We know your love by your gift of Jesus who laid down his life for us. Give us eyes to see the greatness of Jesus in deeper ways. We want to love and trust Jesus our Savior.

In his name,
Amen.

Since the children have flesh and blood,
he too shared in their humanity so that by his death
he might destroy him who holds the power of death — that
is, the devil — and free those who all their lives were held in
slavery by their fear of death.

HEBREWS 2:14, 15

REFLECT ON THE TEACHING

What is it saying? (Put this verse in your own words.)

WORSHIP

What have I learned that I can praise God for?

REPENTANCE

How do I fail to realize this truth in my life?

What am I like when I forget this truth?
(What do I feel? How do I act? How do I treat God and others?)

THANKFULNESS FOR A SAVIOR

How is Jesus the ultimate example of someone who lived out the truth of this verse?

How is Jesus' death on the cross the ultimate payment for this sin or need of mine?

ASPIRATION

How does this verse show me what I should be or do?

How would I be different if this truth were powerfully real to me? (Ask God for it!)

OBJECTIVES

1. *To understand the qualities needed to resist temptation.*

Jesus is often thought of as a super hero. He resisted the devil because he is God. But we are mere mortals. We fail because we are human. It takes a super hero to defeat a super-human villain.

The account of Jesus' temptation does not jive with this view. Jesus was weak when the devil came to him. He was hungry and alone in a desert. What followed was not a display of miraculous power. Instead, Jesus remained utterly dependent upon his Father. He was like a child who does what his father tells him to do when a stranger comes offering a candy bar. He turns and runs because he trusts his father's words, not because he is exceptionally good at resisting chocolate.

Jesus was more humble than we are, and that is why he was able to resist the devil. It is our pride, our strength that makes us fall, not our frailty. Jesus did not look at his circumstances or his experience to decide whether or not to trust His Father. Instead, he believed every word his Father spoke. When the devil pointed out that the Father did not look like he cared about his starving Son, Jesus replied that he did not need bread to know that his Father loved him. His Father had said, "This is my beloved Son in whom I am well pleased." What was bread when compared to that?

The source of true obedience is trust. It is found in the humble, childlike heart, that believes what the Father has promised, not the proud, unbelieving heart that wants to prove his or her worthiness. In his second temptation, the devil told Jesus to prove the authenticity of his faith by putting himself at risk. Jesus knew that if he complied, he would be proving the opposite. He did not need to see his Father's protection in order to trust him. Faith is being certain of what we do not see (Hebrews 11:1). Jesus' confidence in His Father's care came from God's promises alone. It was his humble confidence in his Father that made the devil's temptation weightless. Jesus obeyed because he knew his Father and lived by his every word.

The first two temptations reveal the devil's desire. He wants to lead us away from a humble trust in our Father's promises. He wants us to trust in what we can do or see. The devil did not tempt Jesus to do something flagrantly immoral. Instead he tempted him to provide for his own needs. Food and safety are basic human needs. It is here that we will be tempted as well. When the paycheck is small or absent, will our Father provide as he promised? As society gets more dangerous, will our Father protect us and our families? The devil will try to turn us away from God's promises and move us toward finding independent ways to care for ourselves. Will we believe our Father and submit to his will, or doubt his commitment to us and take matters into our own hands?

It is our pride that makes us easy prey for the devil. We think we can take better care of ourselves and our loved ones than God can. We think we are better interpreters of our circumstances than he is. We find our identity in our performance rather than God's declaration. Jesus was humble. He never used his power to prove his identity, or to provide for his own safety or comfort. He trusted his Father completely and was never disappointed.

The final temptation seems more like Satan. Inflaming the lust for fame, power and wealth is what we expect him to do. But Jesus is King of the earth. Someday every knee will bow to him. So, Satan was not offering Jesus anything that was not his right to possess. He was merely offering a pain-free way for Jesus to obtain the kingdom that was rightfully his.

Jesus' answer reveals the key to his sinless heart. Jesus genuinely worshipped and served his Father alone! His Father's plan was the cross, not comfort. So, he obeyed his Father and went to the cross. He knew that to worship and serve anyone other than his Father would be horrific, even if it brought wealth, fame and every luxury know to man. Paul explained the attitude behind Jesus' obedience:

Your attitude should be the same as that of Christ Jesus:

Who, being in very nature God,
did not consider equality with God something to be grasped,
but made himself nothing,
taking the very nature of a servant,
being made in human likeness.
And being found in appearance as a man,
he humbled himself
and became obedient to deathó
even death on a cross!
Philippians 2:5-8

In his season of temptation, it was Jesus' humility, his "making himself nothing," that made the devil's offers look as empty as they were. Jesus loved his Father's will more than he loved his own life.

Being weak is the secret to resisting temptation. When we are weak, we run to our Father. We trust him, rather than ourselves. But, we fail time and time again! Our Father knows we need someone to pass the test in our place. That is why he sent his Son. As Dr. Keller says, "Jesus did not resist temptation merely to give us an example. He did it to give us a record." The moment we put our faith in Jesus, we were credited with his obedience. We never need to fear our Father's displeasure or rejection. Because of Jesus alone, his declaration over each of us is, "This is my child, whom I love. In him/her I am well pleased." We can trust our Father's words!

Theological Concept

The cross.

The cross is the most significant event in history. From the human point of view it looked like the end of a short career for one more man who claimed to be the "Messiah." The crowds came, saw him die, and went home. Even his disciples viewed Jesus' death as the tragic end to all that they had hoped for. Jesus had spoken about his death and resurrection, but it did not seem possible that the one who quieted a hurricane with a simple command, or who raised the dead by saying "get up, little girl" could die like that. Nor did it seem necessary. From their perspective, Jesus made a tragic mistake.

From God's perspective, however, something else was happening!

"God was reconciling the world to himself in Christ, not counting men's sins against them" (2 Corinthians 5:19).

"God made him who had no sin to be sin for us, so that in him we might become the righteousness of God" (2 Corinthians 5:21).

We, too, can miss what happened on the cross. Some say that the cross shows how much God loves us. But Jesus showed incredible love simply by becoming a man and dwelling among us. He healed the sick, raised the dead, welcomed the outcast. If the cross was just a display of love, it was a poor one. It is silly to die just for show.

Jesus was not a masochist. He did not want to die on the cross unless it was absolutely necessary. At Gethsemane he cried out, "My Father, if it is not possible for this cup to be taken away unless I drink it, may your will be done" (Matthew 26:42).

Jesus agonized over his upcoming death. There was something so horrible about the cross that utterly terrified him. What was the 'cup' that scared him so badly? Jesus, whose thoughts were steeped in Scripture, was referring to a cup spoken about in the Psalms and Prophets.

But it is God who judges:

He brings one down, he exalts another.
In the hand of the LORD is a cup
full of foaming wine mixed with spices;
he pours it out, and all the wicked of the earth
drink it down to its very dregs.
Psalm 75:7, 8

Awake, awake!
Rise up, O Jerusalem,
you who have drunk from the hand of the LORD
the cup of his wrath,
you who have drained to its dregs
the goblet that makes men stagger.
Isaiah 51:17
(see also Jer 25:15; Ezekiel 23:31-33; Habakkuk 2:16.)

The cup was the symbol of God's wrath against man's sin. God hates evil. He does not overlook what Adam and Eve and their offspring have done. Adam and Eve not only disobeyed, they rebelled and then blamed God and others for their own sin. We do the same. God cannot call evil good. He is pure. The cup of God's wrath is not a cup of his irritability or impatience. Instead, it is real justice for real evil. God must judge evil and condemn it. So the cup of his wrath has been prepared.

But God loves guilty, hard hearted, sinners whom he created in his image. All of us have a terrible cup of judgment facing us which could never have been removed unless Jesus was willing to drink it for us.

The cross was not one of many ways for God to save his people. If there was any other way, Jesus would have been spared. Why was the cross the only way? Jesus, himself, the innocent Son of God, took our place before God. He 'became' our sin. As our sin bearer, he cried out "My God! Why have you forsaken me?" Jesus did not just feel forsaken, he was forsaken. Jesus was utterly cast away, repulsive to his Father, condemned as an enemy. Jesus drank our cup to the dregs. The cup of judgment is empty for those who put their faith in the One who drank it in their place. God has no condemnation or anger left to give us. It was all given to Christ.

But that is not all that the cross accomplished. Jesus earned a cup of blessing. God is just. He must reward such self-sacrificing love, such faithful trust in his Father. This is the cup we now drink. The reward for Jesus is eternal life. Death cannot come to anyone as righteous as Jesus. Therefore, if we are in Jesus, we cannot die. Our bodies may die, but we will live forever with Jesus, in new bodies — imperishable, immortal, glorious (1 Corinthians 15:42-58).

Why would Jesus die for us? What did he get for all his pain? He only got one thing: us! Hebrews 12:2 tells us that Jesus had joy set before him as he endured the cross. We were his joy! There was no other reason to die in our place. Some argue that God's motive in sending the Son to die was to reveal his own glory. But what is God's glory? The glory of God is his incomprehensible love for sinful people. His glory is the price he was willing to pay to uphold justice and still bring his beloved sons and daughters home.

In the last chapter we saw that Jesus was the One who would crush the Serpent's head. Now let's look at how he defeated the enemy.

Jesus looked like an ordinary boy, but he lived like no child of Adam ever had. The Serpent tried to deceive him like he had deceived Eve and her offspring. But he quickly discovered that he was outmatched!

Remember how the Serpent began his temptation of Eve. He planted doubts in her mind about God's love for her. He did the same with all Eve's descendents. It always worked — until Jesus.

What do the following verses reveal about Jesus' relationship with his Father? What did he know about his Father's heart? Write your answers after each verse.

> JOHN 3:35   The Father loves the Son and has placed everything in his hands.
> *Jesus knew that his Father loved him.*

> JOHN 5:20   For the Father loves the Son and shows him all he does.
> *Jesus always knew his Father's love and trusted him to lead him in every circumstance.*

> JOHN 17:20-23   My prayer is not for them alone. I pray also for those who will believe in me through their message, that all of them may be one, Father, just as you are in me and I am in you. May they also be in us so that the world may believe that you have sent me. I have given them the glory that you gave me, that they may be one as we are one: I in them and you in me. May they be brought to complete unity to let the world know that you sent me and have loved them even as you have loved me.
> *Jesus knew that his Father had always loved him. The Father was in Jesus, and they were in complete unity.*

> JOHN 6:27   Do not work for food that spoils, but for food that endures to eternal life, which the Son of Man will give you. On him God the Father has placed his seal of approval.
> *Jesus knew that his Father approved of him.*

Sometimes we think that Jesus possessed a supernatural willpower that enabled him to resist Satan. This is not what the Bible teaches. Jesus trusted his Father's heart. That is why He never sinned!

Satan came to Jesus just like he came to Eve. This time the setting was a desert wasteland, not a garden.

> MATTHEW 3:16-4:11   As soon as Jesus was baptized, he went up out of the water. At that moment heaven was opened, and he saw the Spirit of God descending like a dove and lighting on him. And a voice from heaven said, "This is my Son, whom I love; with him I am well pleased." Then Jesus was led by the Spirit into the desert to be tempted by the devil. After fasting forty days and forty nights, he was hungry. The tempter came to him and said, "If you are the Son of God, tell these stones to become bread." Jesus answered, "It is written: 'Man does not live on bread alone, but on every word that comes from the mouth of God.'" Then the devil took him to the holy city and had him stand on the highest point of the temple. "If you are the Son of God," he said, "throw yourself down. For it is written: 'He will command his angels concerning you, and they will lift you up in their hands, so that you will not strike your foot against a stone.'" Jesus answered him, "It is also written: 'Do not put the Lord your God to the test.'" Again, the devil took him to a very high mountain and showed him all the kingdoms of the world and their splendor. "All this I will give you," he said, "if you will bow down and worship me." Jesus said to him, "Away from me, Satan! For it is written: 'Worship the Lord your God, and serve him only.'" Then the devil left him, and angels came and attended him.

→ What did the Father declare from heaven at Jesus' baptism?
The Father declared that Jesus is his Son, whom he loves. He announced that he is well pleased with Jesus.

The devil began his first two temptations with the same seven words.

→ What were they?
If you are the Son of God...

→ What did these words imply about the Father's declaration concerning Jesus?
The devil suggested that the Father's declaration might not be true.

Like Eve, Jesus was put on the defensive. "Did God really say..." was being replaced with "If." Consider the devil's first temptation of Jesus.

➔ What did he tell him to do?
   He told Jesus to tell the stones to become bread.

Once again the devil pretended to be more caring than God. He said nothing directly, but he implied plenty. In essence he said, "Here you are, Jesus, the one whom God 'says' he loves, starving in the wilderness! A real Father does not make his children suffer like this!"

➔ How did Jesus answer?
   Jesus answered, "It is written: 'Man does not live on bread alone, but on every word that comes from the mouth of God.'"

Jesus answered the devil with Scripture. His answer reflected his deepest desire.

➔ What did Jesus love more than bread?
   Jesus loved every word that his Father spoke.

How Jesus loved his Father! Satan's words fell to the ground. But Satan was not ready to give up.

➔ What did he tell Jesus to do in his second temptation?
   "If you are the Son of God," he said, "throw yourself down..."

➔ What was he challenging him to prove?
   He was telling Jesus to prove that his Father would keep his promise to protect him.

We are only tempted to prove something when we are uncertain about it ourselves. Jesus was sure of his Father's protection.

➔ What did he tell the devil?
   Jesus answered him, "It is also written: 'Do not put the Lord your God to the test.'"

Notice that Satan did not tempt Jesus to do something obviously immoral. Instead, he tempted him with bread. Jesus needed food to live. So the devil tempted Jesus to seek his basic human needs from someone else besides his Father. Jesus needed protection. So the devil tempted him to test his Father's commitment to keep his Son safe.

→ What sin are you more likely to commit: indulging in something flagrantly immoral or acting on your own to get your needs met?
Most of us are more likely to act on our own to get our basic needs met.

Obedience is always a matter of trust. Satan had failed to plant any doubt in Jesus' mind concerning his Father's love. But he proceeded as if he had. Like he had done with Eve, he enticed Jesus to seek his own glory through an act of disobedience.

→ What did Satan offer Jesus?
Satan offered Jesus all the kingdoms of the world and their splendor.

→ What did Jesus have to do to receive the devil's gift?
Jesus had to bow down and worship the devil.

→ How did Jesus answer the devil?
Jesus said to him, "Away from me, Satan! For it is written: 'Worship the Lord your God, and serve him only.'"

→ When Eve lost sight of God's glory, whose glory did she seek?
Eve sought her own glory.

→ When Jesus kept sight of Father's glory, whose glory did he seek?
Jesus sought his Father's glory.

Take an honest look at your life. Think about the voices you follow, and the deep longings that rule your heart.

➜ Who are you more like, Jesus or Eve?
We are all more like Eve. We lose sight of God's glory and end up seeking our own.

➜ How can this realization show you your continual need for a Savior?
When we see how perfectly Jesus loved and trusted his Father, we see what it means to be genuinely good. When we face how easily we fall for the devil's temptations, we realize that we can never save ourselves. We need a Savior.

➜ What did Jesus command Satan to do?
Jesus commanded him to go away.

➜ What did Satan do?
Satan left him.

Jesus did not banish the devil until he had faced his temptations and utterly defeated him. His suffering and his obedience are part of our rescue.

When Jesus finished his life on earth, he was guiltless. Unlike Adam and Eve (and us), he had no shame to cover, no guilt to hide. But he was like Adam and Eve in one respect. He was a blame shifter! However, instead of shifting personal guilt onto God and others, he shifted sinful mankind's guilt onto himself. Jesus "crushed the Serpent's head" in surprising way. Satan never saw it coming!

> ISAIAH 53:1-6   ¹ Who has believed our message
> and to whom has the arm of the LORD been revealed?
> ² He grew up before him like a tender shoot,
> and like a root out of dry ground.
> He had no beauty or majesty to attract us to him,
> nothing in his appearance that we should desire him.
> ³ He was despised and rejected by men,
> a man of sorrows, and familiar with suffering.
> Like one from whom men hide their faces
> he was despised, and we esteemed him not.
> ⁴ Surely he took up our infirmities
> and carried our sorrows,
> yet we considered him stricken by God,

smitten by him, and afflicted.
⁵ But he was pierced for our transgressions,
he was crushed for our iniquities;
the punishment that brought us peace was upon him,
and by his wounds we are healed.
⁶ We all, like sheep, have gone astray,
each of us has turned to his own way;
and the LORD has laid on him
the iniquity of us all.

➜ According to these verses, what have we done against God? (vs. 5, 6)
We have broken his Law and done what is evil. We have turned to our own way, like sheep who refuse to follow their shepherd.

➜ How did we treat Jesus when he came? (vs. 2-4)
We were not attracted to him, nor did we desire him. We despised and rejected him. When he suffered for our sins, we thought he was getting what he deserved from God.

➜ Why was Jesus pierced and crushed?
He suffered to pay for our transgressions.

➜ What did his punishment bring us?
He brought us peace.

➜ What did his wounds do for us?
His wounds healed us.

➜ According to verse 6 what have we all done?
We have left the Shepherd of our souls.

➜ Whose sin (iniquity) was laid upon Jesus?
The sin of us all was laid upon Jesus.

HEBREWS 2:14   Since the children have flesh and blood, he too shared in their humanity so that by his death he might destroy him who holds the power of death — that is, the devil...

→ What did Jesus do to destroy the devil?
He died.

Jesus lived the life we have never lived. Not once did he doubt his Father's heart, or allow himself to be deceived by the suggestions of the devil. Jesus earned his Father's warm embrace and a rich entrance into heaven, but he did not get it. Instead of an embrace, Jesus was crushed and punished for our rebellion and unbelief. He suffered so that we could receive the warm welcome he earned.

God did not pass over Adam and Eve's guilt or believe their excuses. He does not pass over our guilt or believe our excuses. There is only one remedy for our sin, the cross. Jesus was willing to stand in our place and receive our punishment.

We do not need to be afraid of life or death. The devil wants to see us exposed and condemned. But he will not get what he desires. Jesus was condemned in our place. If we belong to Jesus, we always have the Father's smile.

MEDITATION

The cross demonstrates the incomprehensible love of God for his people. Yet, in order for his love to transform you personally, you have to know that God had you in mind when he sent Jesus to the cross.

> *But he was pierced for our transgressions,*
> *he was crushed for our iniquities;*
> *the punishment that brought us peace was upon him,*
> *and by his wounds we are healed.*
>
> ISAIAH 53:5

PRAYER

Father,

You are worthy of my heart's worship. I do not have to pretend or waste my time trying to convince you that I'm better than I am. You know the real me. You sent your Son to my rescue. You cursed him in my place. Seeing Jesus lifted up on the cross convinces me that you care. You are not blind or naïve about sin. But you love sinners like me.

Make this truth real to my soul. Cause it to go deep into my heart and transform my view of you. The cross is where you draw me in, and I want to be drawn with all my heart.

In Jesus' name,
Amen.

But he was pierced for our transgressions,
he was crushed for our iniquities;
the punishment that brought us peace was upon him,
and by his wounds we are healed.

ISAIAH 53:5

REFLECT ON THE TEACHING

What is it saying? (Put this verse in your own words.)

WORSHIP

What have I learned that I can praise God for?

REPENTANCE

How do I fail to realize this truth in my life?

What am I like when I forget this truth?
(What do I feel? How do I act? How do I treat God and others?)

THANKFULNESS FOR A SAVIOR

How is Jesus the ultimate example of someone who lived out the truth of this verse?

How is Jesus' death on the cross the ultimate payment for this sin or need of mine?

ASPIRATION

How does this verse show me what I should be or do?

How would I be different if this truth were powerfully real to me? (Ask God for it!)

OBJECTIVE

To discern the difference between believing and behaving.

Doesn't the Bible teach us to obey God and keep his commands? Don't God's commands matter? The apostle Paul gives us a clear answer. The Law is good. But we are not.

So then, the law is holy, and the commandment is holy, righteous and good.

Did that which is good, then, become death to me? By no means! But in order that sin might be recognized as sin, it produced death in me through what was good, so that through the commandment sin might become utterly sinful.

We know that the law is spiritual; but I am unspiritual, sold as a slave to sin (Romans 7:12-14).

The Law is designed to expose our sin. It kills us because we cannot keep it. When we make a commitment to obey the Law at any point, we become aware of something inside us that demands its own way. The Law says "Do not covet." But when we try to comply, we find ourselves coveting everything in sight.

We get worse, not better when we try to keep God's commands on our own. We hate failing! But failure is an important step in our sanctification. If we don't let the Law reveal our slavery to sin, we will never see our ongoing need for a Savior.

The Galatians stopped needing their Savior. They abandoned the One who rescued them and turned to legalism. Legalists appear to love God's law, but instead they avoid God's law and turn to rituals and traditions.

God's Law is summed up by two commandments: Love the Lord your God with all your heart and with all your soul and with all your mind and with all your strength. Love your neighbor as yourself (Mark 12:30). No one can perform this kind of love. But we can keep smaller, more manageable laws. It is to these we run when we are abandoning Christ. Obedience for the "foolish" Galatians became a matter of being circumcised, only eating with Jews (2:12), and observing days, months, seasons and years (3:10). Their motives for obedience were pleasing people and boasting in their performance (1:10, 5:13).

We are no different from the Galatians. Today, we have our own list of behaviors that make us feel like good Christians, and keep those in our Christian subculture happy. Most of them have little or nothing to do with loving God or our neighbor. Legalists behave in order to avoid exposure.

Believing is the opposite of behaving. If we believe the message of the cross we will be utterly transformed, but our eyes will not be on ourselves. Believing is for those of us who have recognized, on some level, that we cannot perform anything of value. We need the cross. Jesus must take away our guilt and provide a record or we will perish.

Believing the Gospel leads to humility and gratitude. Our boast is the cross alone (Galatians 5:

14). Behaving leads to pride or envy, depending upon how well we are doing in comparison to others (Galatians 5:26). Believers have their eyes on Christ. Behavers have their eyes on themselves and their audience. We cannot mix believing the Gospel and trusting in our own works.

The book exchange described in the study exposes the truth about hearts. If anyone were to write our real life story, including every thought, every word, and every deed, we would be mortified and ashamed. The secret envy, the self-centered demands, the silent assessments we have made of others are appalling. We keep our true selves hidden for a good reason! Only when we face the truth about ourselves, we will cry out for a Savior.

Jesus has nothing to hide. He never said a word that was not full of truth and grace. He never had a stray moment of self absorption, not a second of envy, nor a trace of malice. Jesus is the perfect beauty, inside and out.

A life of faith is an honest life. We look at our own hearts and can say with Paul, "I know that nothing good dwells in me, that is, in my flesh" (Romans 7:18). Then we run to the cross and also say with Paul, "May I never boast except in the cross of our Lord Jesus Christ, through which the world has been crucified to me, and I to the world" (Galatians 6:14).

THEOLOGICAL CONCEPT

The Holy Spirit.

If we try to hang on to the message of the Gospel in our own strength, we will fail. God has sent his Spirit into our hearts to encourage our faith. The Holy Spirit is the third person in the Trinity (Matthew 28:19). He is fully God, like the Father and the Son. As God promised to send the "seed of the woman," he also promised to send his Holy Spirit into our hearts.

I will give them an undivided heart and put a new spirit in them; I will remove from them their heart of stone and give them a heart of flesh. Then they will follow my decrees and be careful to keep my laws. They will be my people, and I will be their God (Ezekiel 11:19-20).

I will sprinkle clean water on you, and you will be clean; I will cleanse you from all your impurities and from all your idols. I will give you a new heart and put a new spirit in you; I will remove from you your heart of stone and give you a heart of flesh. And I will put my Spirit in you and move you to follow my decrees and be careful to keep my laws (Ezekiel 36:25-28.).

God sent Jesus to take away our guilt and to give us a new record. He sent his Holy Spirit to give us new hearts that would believe the Gospel and be transformed from the inside out. Jesus said it was better for us to have the Holy Spirit in our hearts, than for us to have Jesus' own physical presence.

"Now I am going to him who sent me, yet none of you asks me, 'Where are you going?' Because I have said these things, you are filled with grief. But I tell you the truth: It is for your good that I am going away. Unless I go away, the Counselor will not come to you; but if I go, I will send him to you. When he comes, he will convict the world of guilt in regard to sin and righteousness and judgment: in regard to sin, because men do not believe in me; in regard to righteousness, because I am going to the Father, where you can see me no longer; and in regard to judgment, because the prince of this world now stands condemned (John 16:5-11).

Notice the sin that the Holy Spirit reveals. It is not the sin of a poor performance, but the sin of refusing to believe in Jesus. The Holy Spirit testifies about Jesus to our own hearts (John 15:26) and reminds us of all that Jesus taught while he lived among us (John 14:26).

We grow as Christians by continuing to believe the Gospel through the power of the Holy Spirit. We must not forsake faith by running to our performances. The Holy Spirit does not come to behavers, but to believers (Galatians 3:1-3). The Holy Spirit wonderfully encourages our faith and enables us to enjoy our relationship with God, our Father. (Romans 8:15-17). Without the Holy Spirit we could not believe the Gospel. But the Holy Spirit is in the heart of every believer, helping us to lay hold of Christ in our weakness (Romans 8:26, 27).

The cross is not something we can put behind us. In fact, as we grow in our faith, our comprehension of the cross must grow as well. Why? Because we forget. We forget the price Jesus paid to remove our guilt and shame, and we try to remove it ourselves through our efforts. As Rose Marie Miller says, "Our heart always wants a record!" We would rather trust in what we can see — a better performance, a sign of our own maturity; rather than in what we cannot see — the cross of Christ.

The apostle Paul was distressed by a group of believers in Galatia who were doing this very thing.

> GALATIANS 1:6   I am astonished that you are so quickly deserting the one who called you by the grace of Christ and are turning to a different gospel...

> GALATIANS 2:21   I do not set aside the grace of God, for if righteousness could be gained through the law, Christ died for nothing!

➜ According to Paul, is it possible for Christians to desert Jesus?
Yes. The Galatian Christians were deserting Jesus.

➜ How? What do they set aside? What do they seek?
They set aside the grace of God and seek to gain their own righteousness by keeping the law.

➜ If we try to earn a record through keeping the law, what do we do with Christ's death?
We act like he died for nothing. We assert that the cross was not necessary, since we think we can keep God's law well enough to please him on our own.

➜ How have you set aside God's grace and tried to obtain a righteousness of your own through performance?
Answers will vary. The answer is usually tied to our reputations. For example, mothers can set aside God's grace by trying to become a perfect parent, doing whatever it takes to produce perfect kids. Her "verdict" comes from doing whatever "good mothers" do and from raising kids who make her look like a "good mother."

Seeing the sinful ways we try to obtain our own righteousness will not bring change. Our hearts long for something perfect to delight in. That perfection resides in Christ alone.

> 2 CORINTHIANS 5:21   God made him who had no sin to be sin for us, so that in him we might become the righteousness of God.

This verse describes an exchange. Something marred is traded for something perfect.

Imagine that your every thought, word and deed from the past week has been written down accurately and in detail. This record has been published and is on the New York Times bestseller list. Think carefully about your week. Have you gossiped, judged, envied, lied, yelled? Did you have any thoughts you would rather keep secret?

➜ If all were to be exposed in print, how would you feel? How sinless are you?
  We all have thoughts, words and actions that we would hate for anyone to see.

> 1 JOHN 1:5   God is light; in him there is no darkness at all.

From all eternity Jesus never had a single thought or spoke a single word that could not stand complete exposure. There is no hidden malice, not even the first hint of deception or envy. Stop for a moment and ponder this amazing truth about Jesus.

2 Corinthians 5:21 describes a book exchange of sorts. The book which records my heart and actions receives the title, One Week in the Life of Jesus Christ. All my shameful thoughts, words and deeds are exposed; only they are written as if they describe the heart, mind and mouth of Christ. He becomes me in this book.

➜ What must it have felt like for Jesus to become sin?
  We can barely stand the memory of the awful things we have believed, said or done. Jesus must have loathed every second that he wore our sin.

➜ When did this exchange of records actually happen?
  Jesus wore our sin on the cross.

Having my sin removed by Jesus is a wonderful thing. But it is not enough. I need something more. And God gives me much more. According to 2 Corinthians 5:21, a second book is published entitled, One Week in the Life of Sue Cortese. As I read through the first few pages, the beauty of this life astonishes me. There is wisdom, justice and self-sacrificing love. Compassion, gentleness and humility are combined with great courage and boldness. I see an unwavering trust in the Father that resists every temptation of the devil.

→ Whose life am I reading about?
The life of Christ.

→ According to 2 Corinthians 5:21, what do we "become" in Christ?
We become the righteousness of Christ.

→ How does it feel to realize that all of Christ's beautiful righteousness has been credited to you?
Jesus' righteousness is the perfection we all long to attain. When we are in him, we are not only seen as flawless, but as utterly perfect people.

The moment you put your trust in Christ, his righteousness became yours forever.

What does it mean to "become" the righteousness of Christ? We gain understanding about the nature of this righteousness from the book of Romans.

> ROMANS 4:5, 6   However, to the man who does not work but trusts God
> who justifies the wicked, his faith is credited as righteousness. David says the
> same thing when he speaks of the blessedness of the man to whom God credits
> righteousness apart from works.

→ Are these verses talking about something we did in the past, or something we do now?
It is something we do now.

→ Is this righteousness something that turns us into sinless people, or something God credits to wicked people who trust him?
This righteousness is credited to wicked people. It is given to people who cannot perform righteous works.

→ What does it mean to have something credited to you?
You receive something which you did not earn.

→ What does it mean to have God's righteousness credited to you?
It means that the very righteousness of God is on my record, as if I had lived a life as beautiful as Jesus'.

What does it mean to "not work"? It means we stop working to improve our book, and instead trust in Christ's book, which has been credited to us. It means every morning we remember the exchange of the cross. When we recognize our moral failures and lack of faith, it means we do not run to performances and resolutions to become people who do not sin. Instead, with humble gratitude, we run to the cross — amazed by the love of God for sinners like us.

→ How much does the Father delight in Christ?
The Father's delight in Jesus is full and unwavering.

→ If his perfection is credited to you, how much does the Father delight in you right now?
The Father delights in all who have the righteousness of Jesus credited into their account by faith. His delight for us matches the delight he has for his son.

MEDITATION

As always, the only way Jesus' sacrifice will transform you is to realize that he loved you, personally. He died with your name on his lips. As you meditate this week, focus on the personal pronoun, "me."

I have been crucified with Christ and I no longer live,
but Christ lives in me.
The life I live in the body, I live by faith in the
Son of God, who loved ME and gave himself for ME.
GALATIANS 2:20

PRAYER

Father,

Your Son is beautiful in his perfection. He lived to give me a perfect life story. He died to take away my shameful life story. If you could look at my life and embrace what I do and say, you would not be just or good. But if you demanded of me a life I could never live, you would not be loving. Thank you for placing my sins upon Christ at the cross, so that by faith I could have his righteousness placed upon me. Let me turn away from my own righteousness, and glory in the righteousness of Christ alone.

In Jesus' name,
Amen.

I have been crucified with Christ and I no longer live,
but Christ lives in me.
The life I live in the body, I live by faith in the
Son of God, who loved me and gave himself for me.

GALATIANS 2:20

REFLECT ON THE TEACHING

What is it saying? (Put this verse in your own words.)

WORSHIP

What have I learned that I can praise God for?

REPENTANCE

How do I fail to realize this truth in my life?

What am I like when I forget this truth?
(What do I feel? How do I act? How do I treat God and others?)

Thankfulness for a Savior

How is Jesus the ultimate example of someone who lived out the truth of this verse?

How is Jesus' death on the cross the ultimate payment for this sin or need of mine?

Aspiration

How does this verse show me what I should be or do?

How would I be different if this truth were powerfully real to me? (Ask God for it!)

PART THREE ✤ LIVING BY FAITH

OBJECTIVE

1. *To recognize our agendas and surrender them for the "one thing."*

Martha was a performer. Her heart's desire was to bring Jesus something worthy of his admiration and gratitude. Her work was not an expression of her thankfulness for Jesus, but an effort to obtain his appreciation for her. She wanted Jesus' love on her terms. She would perform, and Jesus would notice, care, and see to it that she had all the help she needed.

Jesus' response to her was stunning. He told Martha that her problem was that she was worried and distracted about things that did not matter. What were those things? Her labor in the kitchen. The meal. It would have been easy to argue with Jesus. Her labor did matter! They needed to eat. She was taking care of the most important thing. But Jesus' value system is the opposite of ours. Mary chose the ONE thing that mattered — listening to every word that proceeded out of the mouth of her Lord.

Like Martha, we believe that our agendas are urgent. The more "godly" they are, the harder it is to believe that they are not the one thing that matters. From Christian ministry to taking care of our families, we easily become consumed with our labor and forget the Gospel. We worry and fret. We become critical of those who are not helping and of God who seems distant and unconcerned. We see ourselves as martyrs, doing all the work while others sit and do nothing. No one seems to care.

But Jesus knows our real problem. We have not chosen the one thing that matters. Jesus is the thing. Until we believe the Gospel, our labor is a distraction. We remain utterly self focused, wanting Jesus and others to submit to our agenda.

This story is full of the good news of the Gospel. We cannot abandon our agendas on our own. Jesus must convert us. How did he convert Martha? He melted her heart. When he repeated her name, he let her know that he loved her.

Martha's demandingness and unbelief did not hinder Jesus' love for her. Our sin does not hinder his love for us, either. When Jesus visited Martha's home, he was on his way to Jerusalem to die for her and for us. God's grace for sinners can melt the most stubborn heart. But each of us must hear Jesus saying our name twice, before we can respond to him. Until we know he loves us intimately, by grace alone, we will always run to our duties and performances to feel valuable and secure. But when we hear his voice reminding us of his unfailing love, we will accept his invitation to join Mary at his feet.

FROM WORRY TO REST

It can be hard to imagine what living by faith looks like. What do we do? What do we stop doing? There is a scene from the Bible that draws a sharp contrast between a life of faith and a life of performance. It is the story of Mary and Martha on the day when they welcomed Jesus into their home.

> LUKE 10:38-42   As Jesus and his disciples were on their way, he came to a village where a woman named Martha opened her home to him. She had a sister called Mary, who sat at the Lord's feet listening to what he said. But Martha was distracted by all the preparations that had to be made. She came to him and asked, "Lord, don't you care that my sister has left me to do the work by myself? Tell her to help me!"
>
> "Martha, Martha," the Lord answered, "you are worried and upset about many things, but only one thing is needed. Mary has chosen what is better, and it will not be taken away from her."

Martha and Mary both loved Jesus. He loved both sisters. But Mary listened, while Martha served. When Jesus did not support Martha, she became upset.

➜ What do Martha's words reveal about her perception of Jesus?
  Martha believed that Jesus did not care.

➜ How was Martha's view of God similar to Eve's?
  Both Martha and Eve believed that God did not care about them.

Did Jesus care about Martha? Yes! When Jesus stopped at Martha's home, he was on his way to Jerusalem to die for her. He loved Martha much more than she realized.

➜ According to Martha, what was the problem? (What did she say?)
  Mary had left Martha to do all the work by herself. Jesus did not care or intervene.

→ What did Martha think that Jesus ought to do?
Martha thought that Jesus ought to make Mary get up and help her.

→ What did Jesus say Martha's problem was?
Martha was upset and distracted by many things and had forgotten the one thing that mattered.

→ How similar were Martha and Jesus' perceptions of the real problem? Who was right?
They were completely opposite. Jesus was right.

→ Why wouldn't Jesus tell Mary to help Martha?
Because Mary had chosen the best thing, and Jesus would not take it away from her.

→ Describe a situation in which you feel like you are being treated unfairly.
Answers will vary. (If you, as a leader, describe a current or recent situation, it will create a safe atmosphere for others to do the same.)

→ What are the "many things" that trouble you in this situation?
Answers will vary.

→ When you pray about this situation, what are you asking Jesus to do?
Usually we want Jesus to take away our problems.

➜ According to this passage, what would Jesus consider to be your real problem?
Jesus would consider my real problem to be the many worries and troubles which choke out my faith in Christ.

➜ What is the "one thing" that matters?
Jesus is the one thing. This includes all that Jesus is for us, and all that he has taught us concerning himself.

It is hard to believe that Jesus is the only thing that matters. Life is stressful and there seems to be plenty to worry about. Our performance feels like the one thing that matters. So much hinges on what we do and how well we do it!

How can we be converted to Jesus' point of view? By remembering the cross. Consider Satan's priority for your life. He wants you to doubt God's unfailing love. If you think God is remote and uncaring, you will take care of your concerns your own way. Like Martha, you will place high expectations on yourself and others in order to make life work and get what you think you need. But, like Martha, you will end up feeling alone, misunderstood and unsupported.

God does care and he cannot forget you. Jesus was pursuing Martha even though he appeared to be ignoring her plight. Martha was permitted to fail, and to taste the bitterness that her many worries and troubles created for her. She was angry with Jesus, but he was not angry with her.

➜ What were Jesus' first two words to Martha?
"Martha, Martha."

In English the repetition of a name can express frustration or even anger. But in Hebrew the repetition of a name expresses deep affection and love.

➜ What was the first thing Jesus wanted Martha to know?
Jesus wanted Martha to know that he loved her dearly.

Look again at Martha's situation. She had barged into a room where Jesus was instructing his disciples and their houseguests. She publicly accused Jesus of insensitivity and issued a command. It is unlikely that Martha thought about what she was doing. Suddenly, she was the center of attention. All eyes were on her.

The first thing Jesus did was to let Martha and everyone present know that he felt deep affection for her. This is grace! Jesus' love for Martha was unearned. As she was publicly accusing Jesus, his was publicly affirming his love for her. Those who heard his words would not view Martha as an angry, controlling woman, but as someone their Master loved. Grace is what changes us!

➜ Describe how Jesus' grace toward Martha might change her heart.
Martha would be able to see that Jesus' love for her was not based on her performance or her worthiness. She would realize that he loved her, deeply. Being loved when we are at our worst breaks our pride and makes us long to give our hearts to Jesus.

➜ Take a moment and list some of the things you don't like about yourself.
Answers will vary.

Now, in large letters, write your name twice — covering over all that you have written. This is who you are in God's sight. You are someone who is deeply loved by Jesus. And it is his view of you that matters!

Like Martha, we also have a mental list of our virtues. Martha perceived herself as a competent, dutiful woman who had a better grasp of what needed to happen than Jesus!

➜ Take another moment, to list some of the things about yourself that you take pride in.
Answers will vary.

➜ In large letters, write your name twice, covering all your virtues.

If you belong to Christ, the cross defines you. As Dr. C. John Miller used to say, "Rejoice, you are worse than you think! But God's grace is greater than you dare to believe!" Martha was worse than she thought! Her sin was much bigger than she realized. But Jesus' love for her was greater than she ever dreamed. When relentless streams of accusation or shame plague your conscience, say your name out loud two times. When you are swollen with pride, say your name twice. It is Jesus' love for you that gives you your identity.

Jesus affirmed Martha. But, he loved her enough to tell her the truth without compromising.

→ Who was to blame for Martha's outburst?
Martha.

→ Who needed correction, Martha or Mary?
Martha.

As Jesus affirmed Mary's choice, he was also extending an unspoken invitation to Martha.

→ Where did he want Martha to be?
Jesus wanted Martha to join Mary at his feet.

When we hear the truth about ourselves from Jesus, we also hear his invitation. He loves us and wants us to come to him as we are.

MEDITATION

Jesus is full of truth and grace. His words expose our sin, but they also bring hope and an invitation to deeper intimacy with him. We change as we let Jesus' words penetrate our hearts and melt us into people who desire the "one thing."

> *"Martha, Martha," the Lord answered,*
> *"You are worried and upset about many things,*
> *but only one thing is needed.*
> *Mary has chosen what is better,*
> *and it will not be taken away from her."*
> LUKE 10:41, 42

Replace Martha's name with your own as you meditate on these verses.

PRAYER

Father,

I am as worried and upset as Martha was. I have doubted your sovereign, tender care. I have used prayer to tell you what to do instead of letting you speak to my heart.

Yet your steadfast love for me never ceases and your mercies never come to an end. The cross assures me that you love me, even though you know my darkest thoughts. I want to hear the truth from you and receive your grace. As I meditate on Jesus' words to Martha, help me to believe that you alone matter. I want to join Mary at your feet!

In Jesus' name,
Amen.

" _____ , _____ ," *the Lord answered,*
"You are worried and upset about many things,
but only one thing is needed.
Mary has chosen what is better,
and it will not be taken away from her."

LUKE 10:41, 42

REFLECT ON THE TEACHING

What is it saying? (Put this verse in your own words.)

WORSHIP

What have I learned that I can praise God for?

REPENTANCE

How do I fail to realize this truth in my life?

What am I like when I forget this truth?
(What do I feel? How do I act? How do I treat God and others?)

THANKFULNESS FOR A SAVIOR

How is Jesus the ultimate example of someone who lived out the truth of this verse?

How is Jesus' death on the cross the ultimate payment for this sin or need of mine?

ASPIRATION

How does this verse show me what I should be or do?

How would I be different if this truth were powerfully real to me? (Ask God for it!)

OBJECTIVE:

To live under Jesus' smile instead of working for the smile of others.

The American idol of choice is the fear of man. God's approval can seem nice to us, but the approval of certain people feels critical. People are visible, tangible and audible. They smile, frown or roll their eyes in front of us. We feel their embrace or their stiff arm, and we hear their words. When people welcome us into their lives we feel secure and valuable. When they reject us we feel exposed and condemned.

God is invisible. We can't see his face or hear his voice. So, we speculate. Sometimes, when we remember that he is loving, we view him as a heavenly "Mr. Rogers." For a moment we feel good about God. But this kind of God could never transform us. He may appear friendly, but his universal warmth leaves us unknown and unmoved. On the other hand, when we remember that God is powerful and sees all that we do, we tend to view him as Zeus, with a handful of lightening bolts. Neither of these views of God can free us from the craving for human approval.

We need someone to tell us that we matter, that we will not be utterly abandoned and forgotten. We were designed to know the intimate love and affirmation that exists within the Trinity. But, having abandoned the true knowledge of God, we search for that affirmation in the faces of people. Without God's rescue, we will live for the approval of others all of our lives.

How was Mary able to transcend the strong desire for human approval? How could she go against the expectations of her culture and simply sit at Jesus' feet? The difference between Mary and Martha was that Mary knew Jesus' smile, and it was the supreme joy of her life. Martha did not know his smile so she tried to earn it the same way she had earned smiles her whole life. Mary took time to know Jesus, to listen to what he said, and to receive what he had to give her. On that particular day, Jesus was more critical for Mary than anyone or anything else. People would surely accuse Mary of shirking her work, but she did not seem to notice or care. Jesus' smile over her was her ultimate delight. She knew just where he wanted her ñ close to him. So she boldly sat down and drank in his words.

How can we know Jesus' smile like this? How can his smile be certain and powerful to us? We have to listen to him. Accomplishing our agendas always feels more urgent than knowing Jesus' love. But it never is. One day lived in the consciousness of Jesus' smile is a piece of heaven on earth no matter what happens. One day lived with uncertainty and unbelief is a piece of hell, no matter what happens.

The fleeting joy of human approval simply feeds our insecurity. We are only as acceptable as our latest performance. Tomorrow we may fail! Anxiety is a foretaste of hell, just as love, joy, and peace are a foretaste of heaven.

If we want to be like Mary we need to soak ourselves in the Gospel. Mary may not have fully understood the cross, but she comprehended Jesus' heart. Mary knew that Jesus loved her. She enjoyed his love. She was never disappointed. We have received more from Jesus than Mary did. She may have seen his smile, but we can receive Jesus' smile inside our hearts and be filled to overflowing. Mary may have felt his touch, but the Spirit can confirm the Father's love to our hearts so powerfully that we have to be strengthened just to survive the experience (Ephesians 3:14-21). Mary knew Jesus as a Teacher and a healer. We know Jesus as our Savior who went to the cross so we could be members of his family. Jesus laid down his life for us, and now resides in the heart of every true believer.

We can pray for the grace to know Jesus' love more deeply. More importantly, we must listen to him when he tells us he loves us. We must hear him and take the time to savor his words. To live loved is every Christian's privilege and duty. We are loved by the only One who matters. When we grasp this truth, we will not be ruled by people's expectations, but by the incomprehensible love of Jesus.

THEOLOGICAL CONCEPT

Prayer.

When we pray, we need to remember the Gospel. Our greatest need is to know the love of God in Christ. We cannot know his love if we don't listen. As we read the Scripture, we need to pay attention to what our Father is telling us. One way to do this is to talk to him about what he has said. This is prayer. It is a dialogue in which we listen as much as we talk.

When we listen to our Father, we will discover that he wants to give us himself. The greatest gift God can give is himself. As Jesus concluded his teaching on prayer, he said, "How much more will your Father give the Holy Spirit to those who ask him" (Luke 11:13). When we love someone we want to be with him or her. This is how God feels about us! He wants our prayer to be a time of intimacy with him. The Holy Spirit is God's presence in us. It is his gift of himself. This is what we need to ask for when we pray.

We are so prone to seek our own agendas for our own glory. Every day we need to pray that Jesus would convert us to his agenda. In prayer we ask Jesus to make us certain of his Father's smile. We repent of any works we have been using to get our way and to earn his admiration and favor. We talk to our Father about what he has said in his Word, and ask for grace to believe his promises.

When, like Mary, we are convinced that he loves us, we will want to hear everything he says. Our prayer will become a plea for more of him, not for more of his blessing on our performances.

The meditation exercises at the end of each chapter are an excellent way to learn to pray with confidence and intimacy. If you soak yourself in God's promises, listening to him and taking time to think through the implications of what he is telling you, then prayer will become a spontaneous response to God.

Encourage everyone in your group to continue meditating on God's word. We never outgrow our need to listen to him and receive what he has promised. Faith, like manna, has to be gathered every day. Every day we need to listen, to believe, to run to the One who loves us and will never let us go.

A FAITH AFFIRMED

To see what a life of faith looks like, let's consider the woman who chose the "one thing." Faith is not something you can acquire by following prescribed steps. Therefore it can be hard to pinpoint what it looks like. Mary did not perform, but she did some remarkable things because she grasped the glory of Jesus. Several qualities of Mary's faith are listed below.

> LUKE 10:38-42   As Jesus and his disciples were on their way, he came to a village where a woman named Martha opened her home to him. She had a sister called Mary, who sat at the Lord's feet listening to what he said. But Martha was distracted by all the preparations that had to be made. She came to him and asked, "Lord, don't you care that my sister has left me to do the work by myself? Tell her to help me!" "Martha, Martha," the Lord answered, "You are worried and upset about many things, but only one thing is needed. Mary has chosen what is better, and it will not be taken away from her."

1. MARY KNEW THE REAL PERFORMER.
We tend to live our lives as if God were looking down at us from heaven. We are the performers. God is the audience. But Mary was different. Look at her focus.

➜ Who was the performer in Mary's life?
   Jesus.

➜ Who was the audience?
   Mary.

2. MARY LISTENED.
Performers trust their own insights about what needs to happen. Martha knew what Jesus needed to do.

➜ What was Mary doing as she sat at Jesus' feet?
   She was listening to Jesus.

On some level, Mary must have realized that her own heart was too deceitful to trust and that Jesus alone had the words she needed to hear.

Reflect on your own prayer life.

→ Do you spend most of your time asking Jesus to make certain things happen?
Answers will vary. The key is whether we are telling Jesus what we think he needs to do or asking Him to tell us what we need to know and remember. If we are telling Jesus what to do we are like Martha. We think we see our problems clearly and that we know the best solutions. We believe that Jesus ought to see things the way we do...

→ What kinds of things do you want him to do? Why?
Answers will vary. We usually want Jesus to fix us, fix those we live with, and fix our circumstances.

→ How could you begin to listen to God when you pray? (Consider using the meditation questions.)
We could begin to pray back to God the truths he has given us. Using the meditation questions can keep us from overlooking what God has clearly written. We make these verses a matter of prayer for ourselves and others. What Jesus has spoken can become more vivid and tangible than our own ideas and feelings.

3. MARY CAME TO JESUS WITHOUT WORKS.

→ What did Martha's frustration with Mary reveal about the cultural expectations of her time?
Mary was expected to help Martha in the kitchen.

Somehow Mary knew that Jesus wanted her, not her service.

→ How did sitting at Jesus' feet reflect Mary's confidence in his acceptance of her?
Mary risked Jesus' rebuke or rejection. Since she did not bring him any works, she had to trust that he wanted her, not her service.

When we come to Jesus with our performances, we are trying to earn his favor. This is hard to give up. Think back to a time when you were in the presence of someone you greatly admire.

➜ What kind of impression did you want to make?
Answers will vary.

➜ What did you do to try to make a good impression?
Answers will vary.

➜ What was your priority: looking good, or getting to know the other person?
When we are in awe of someone we only care about impressing him or her.

When Jesus came to her home, Martha focused on the things she could do to demonstrate her love for Jesus. Mary was able focus on Jesus, alone. She realized that she did not need to make an impression. Think about your relationship with Jesus.

➜ What do you do to earn his approval?
Answers will vary. (I try to act like I trust him. I try to pray insightful prayers. I try to show him that I am doing my best under the difficult circumstances he has given me.)

➜ How do you try to prove your love for him?
Answers will vary.

➜ How would your relationship with Jesus change if you realized that he does not want your service, but you?
It would free me up to be myself with Jesus. I could talk to him about anything and trust him when life is painful and my circumstances are overwhelming.

Jesus is never drawn to us because of our service or devotion. It is the greatness of his heart that enables him to love us. Mary trusted Jesus' heart. That is why she came to him as she was. She knew he would not turn her away.

4. MARY VALUED JESUS' APPROVAL MORE THAN ANYONE ELSE'S.

Mary must have realized that Martha might not understand what she was doing. Martha appears to have been a woman who made quick judgments and spoke her mind openly. If things had not turned out the way they did, Martha might have stayed angry with Mary. She might have told others how Mary had failed her that day.

➜ What might it have cost Mary to not work that day?
It might have cost Mary her reputation.

➜ Have you ever been the object of gossip? How did it feel?
This is always a very painful experience.

Think about the choices you have made in the past week.

➜ What things have you done to avoid conflict, and to keep others happy with you? Give specific examples.
It will help your group if you can give a specific example that most can relate to. It is so instinctive for us to try to gain recognition or avoid conflict that an example from your own week should not be too hard to recall.

➜ What things have you done to keep from making a bad impression, or to keep from being misunderstood?
Answers will vary.

We cannot simply decide to stop living for the approval of others. Only when Jesus' approval becomes the "one thing" that matters will other's opinions become less important.

➔ How did Jesus show that he approved of Mary?
  He told Martha that Mary had chosen the one thing that mattered. He wanted Mary at his feet and praised her for choosing to be there. He also said that Mary's choice would not be taken away from her. She would not be asked to leave.

➔ What do you think Mary felt as she heard Jesus personally affirming her?
  Mary must have felt a deep sense of value. She mattered to the only One whose opinion matters!

➔ Whose approval had the power to transform Mary: Martha's, or Jesus'?
  Jesus is the only one who can transform us from the inside out. His approval, when deeply pondered and experienced, brings lasting peace, joy, freedom and love.

When we know Jesus' approval, we are never quite the same. Our hearts are drawn to him. His love begins to set us free from the need to earn the approval of others.

5. MARY LET JESUS DEFEND HER.

Think of the last time you were personally accused by someone who misjudged your motives.

➔ How did you feel?
  It is very painful and humiliating.

➔ What did you do?
  Answers will vary.

When Martha accused Mary of neglecting her duty, she remained silent. She did not defend herself but waited to hear what Jesus would say.

→ What do you think Mary felt when she heard Jesus' answer to Martha?
Mary must have felt some degree of fear when Martha publicly accused her. Jesus' words would have reassured her that she was completely safe.

→ How did Jesus protect Mary's reputation in a way she could not have done herself?
Mary's self defense would have been questioned. Jesus' word carried the authority of the Son of God. Throughout the centuries Mary has been held up as a woman who chose the right thing and who comprehended Jesus better than most of her contemporaries.

→ What do we forfeit when we become our own defenders?
We miss out on knowing Jesus' desire and ability to protect us. He is our Savior, but we try to do the job ourselves. We often withdraw in fear or aggressively attack our accusers. We end up feeling alone and unprotected.

Mary learned to trust Jesus because she paid attention to what he did, and listened carefully to what he said. This is what we learn to do as we meditate on Scripture. Mary allowed Jesus' words to penetrate and change her. And what did Mary hear? She heard him express his approval. She heard him defend her, and promise that what she had chosen would never be taken away.

Change is a process. We are all "Marthas" by nature. We dream of the freedom that choosing the "one thing" would bring, but it is elusive. In no time we find ourselves worried and troubled; angry with God and everyone else! What can we do?

In the midst of our worst failures, we can still trust what Jesus did on the cross to cover our shame and to assure us of our Father's loving approval. Living by faith is learning to let Jesus love us as we are. It is recognizing that his favor is more valuable than better circumstances. A life of faith costs us our pride and the approval of others. But it brings intimacy with Jesus and greater joy than this world can ever give. We grow in faith by listening to Jesus and allowing his words to transform us. Jesus is the only hero in the Bible. He is the only answer for the fall. He has crushed the head of our enemy and brought us back into the arms of the Trinity. God always loves us wonderfully well, and his favor brings freedom and delight. God wants nothing less than for you to live each day with the certainty that you are under his smile!

MEDITATION

Hopefully your confidence in God's love has grown as you have meditated on his Word over the past weeks. Jesus wants you to come to him as you are.

> Come to me, all you who are weary and burdened,
> and I will give you rest.
> Take my yoke upon you and learn from me,
> for I am gentle and humble in heart,
> and you will find rest for your souls.
> MATTHEW 11:28, 29

If you want to break free from the need to perform, you have to learn from Jesus. You need to know what he is like. His heart is humble and gentle. He wants to give your weary soul the rest you long for.

PRAYER

Father,

When I see Mary's faith, I am humbled. She grasped the greatness of your love in a way that I have not. When you came to her home, her eyes were on you, not herself. She sat at your feet and listened to every word you spoke. In her eyes, you were the "one thing" that mattered.

Mary's faith was not misplaced. She received her heart's desire. But I am not like Mary. I seem to put my faith in anyone or anything besides you. As a result I am weary and burdened. Yet you love me and want me to come to you as I am. Because of the cross I am not condemned. Give me the grace to learn of Jesus. Let me never stop learning about his heart and his gifts. As I conclude this study, help me to continue meditating on your Word. Jesus is the one thing that matters. I want to live a life of faith in him.

In Jesus' name,
Amen.

Come to me, all you who are weary and burdened,
and I will give you rest.
Take my yoke upon you and learn from me,
for I am gentle and humble in heart,
and you will find rest for your souls.

MATTHEW 11:28, 29

REFLECT ON THE TEACHING

What is it saying? (Put this verse in your own words.)

WORSHIP

What have I learned that I can praise God for?

REPENTANCE

How do I fail to realize this truth in my life?

What am I like when I forget this truth?
(What do I feel? How do I act? How do I treat God and others?)

139

THANKFULNESS FOR A SAVIOR

How is Jesus the ultimate example of someone who lived out the truth of this verse?

How is Jesus' death on the cross the ultimate payment for this sin or need of mine?

ASPIRATION

How does this verse show me what I should be or do?

How would I be different if this truth were powerfully real to me? (Ask God for it!)

REFLECT ON THE TEACHING

What is it saying? (Put this verse in your own words.)

WORSHIP

What have I learned that I can praise God for?

REPENTANCE

How do I fail to realize this truth in my life?

What am I like when I forget this truth?
(What do I feel? How do I act? How do I treat God and others?)

THANKFULNESS FOR A SAVIOR

How is Jesus the ultimate example of someone who lived out the truth of this verse?

How is Jesus' death on the cross the ultimate payment for this sin or need of mine?

ASPIRATION

How does this verse show me what I should be or do?

How would I be different if this truth were powerfully real to me? (Ask God for it!)